THE
—BUSINESS—
PLAN
WORKBOOK

THE
—BUSINESS—
PLAN
WORKBOOK

Colin and Paul Barrow

KOGAN
PAGE

First published in Great Britain in 1988 by
Kogan Page Limited, 120 Pentonville Road,
London N1 9JN

Reprinted 1989 (twice)

British Library Cataloguing in Publication Data

Barrow, Colin
    The business plan workbook.
    1. Business firms. Planning
    I. Title   II. Barrow, Paul
    658.4'012

    ISBN 1–85091–539–3
    ISBN 1–85091–363–3 Pbk

Set by DP Photosetting, Aylesbury, Bucks
Printed and bound in Great Britain by
Biddles Limited, Guildford and King's Lynn

Contents

Introduction

This workbook contains the distilled knowledge of the Enterprise Faculty within the Cranfield School of Management and, more importantly, the experiences of the many hundreds of 'student' entrepreneurs who have taken part in our enterprise programmes.

Business planning is at the core of everything we do with people who come to us at Cranfield, whether it is to start a new business or expand an existing one. Over the years we have developed and tested this method of helping people to research and validate their business ideas, and then to write up a business plan themselves.

Towards the end of each enterprise programme we invite a distinguished panel of senior bankers and venture capital providers to review and criticise each business plan presentation. Their valued comments have not only spurred our entrepreneurs to greater heights, but have given the faculty at Cranfield a privileged insight into the minds and thought processes of the principal providers of capital for new and growing enterprises.

This workbook brings together for the first time the processes and procedures required by the relative novice to write a business plan. Also included throughout are examples from the business plans of entrepreneurs who for the most part have gone on to start up successful enterprises.

In addition, we have included criticisms, warnings, and the experiences of investors and of recently successful entrepreneurs when they have a direct bearing on writing and presenting a business plan.

We don't pretend to have made writing up business plans an easy task – but we do think we have made it an understandable one that is within the grasp of everyone with the determination to succeed.

How to Use the Workbook

The workbook contains 20 assignments which, once completed, should ensure that you have all the information you need to write and present a successful business plan. That is, one that helps to accomplish your objective whether it is to gain a greater understanding of the venture you are proposing to start – its viability – or you want to raise outside money.

The workbook does not set out to be a comprehensive textbook on every business subject – finance, marketing, law etc. Rather it gives an appreciation as to how these subjects should be used to prepare your business plan. The topics covered under each assignment will often pull together ingredients from different 'academic' disciplines. For example, elements of law and marketing will be assembled in the assignment in which you are asked to describe your product and its proprietary position (patents, copyright, design registration etc).

For some of the assignments you will almost certainly need to research outside the material contained in this workbook. However, 'technical' explanations of such subjects as cash flow, market research questionnaire design and break-even analysis are included.

The assignments are contained in seven phases which, as well as having a practical logic to their sequence, will provide you with manageable 'chunks' either to carry out yourself at different times, or to delegate to partners and professional advisers. While it is useful to make use of as much help as you can get in preparing the groundwork, you should orchestrate the information and write up the business plan yourself. After all, it is your future that is at stake – and every prospective financier will be backing you and your ability to put this plan into action, not your scriptwriter.

The seven phases are:

- *Phase 1: History and Position to Date*
Here you should describe your business or business idea so far as you have already developed it. In particular, explain your aims, objectives and eventual aspirations.

Introduce your management team, yourself included, and show how your skills and experiences relate to this venture.

Describe your product or service, its current state of development or readiness for the market, and whether or not you have any proprietary rights such as a patent, copyright or registered design.

- *Phase 2: Collection of Data*

This involves identifying the data needed both to validate your business idea and to decide upon the best start-up or growth strategy. In this phase you will be encouraged to gather market research data from as many sources as possible. Particular emphasis will be laid on researching customer needs, market segments and competitors' strengths and weaknesses. The appropriate research methodology and data sources are also described.

- *Phase 3: Developing a Business Strategy*

This involves planning how you will operate each element of your business, based upon the information collected and analysed in earlier phases. In relation to your chosen product or service, the market segment(s) you plan to serve, and the competitive situation, you will decide on such factors as price, promotion, location, and channels of distribution.

- *Phase 4: Operations*

This involves detailing all the activities required to make your strategy happen. It will include such subjects as manufacturing, purchasing, selling, employing people, legal matters and insurance. Your business plan must demonstrate that you have taken account of all the principal matters that concern the operations of your venture.

- *Phase 5: Forecasting Results*

Based on the strategy evolved so far, in this phase you will carry out assignments enabling you to forecast the expected results of your venture. Projections will be made showing likely sales volume and value, pro forma profit and loss, a cash flow forecast and balance sheet, and a break-even analysis.

Although these first five phases are shown in sequence here and in the workbook, in practice you would expect to move backwards and forwards from phase to phase, as a result of new information or a modification of your earlier ideas.

- *Phase 6: Business Controls*

Here you must demonstrate how you will keep track of your business, both as a whole and for each individual element. As well as a bookkeeping system you will need sales and market planning records, customer record cards, personnel files and production control information.

● *Phase 7: Writing Up and Presenting Your Business Plan*
The workbook assignments, when completed, are not your business plan. They are intended to help you to assemble the information needed to write up your business plan. The plan will require substantial editing and rewriting; the way in which it is written up will undoubtedly influence the chances of getting a hearing, if you are seeking outside support for your venture.

Finally, you must give some thought as to how you will handle the meeting with your bank, venture capital house or other backers. Presentation skills and good planning will all help to make for a good 'production', and showbiz counts for a surprising amount in the money world.

Here are some guidelines to help you and your colleagues to complete the business plan assignments:

1. Each assignment will contain:

   ● An introduction or brief description of the content and purpose of the assignment, usually broken down into two or more stages.
   ● Examples as to how other entrepreneurs have answered or commented on parts of the assignment.
   ● An explanation or amplification of any technical topics that need to be understood immediately.

   At the end there is an assignment worksheet with some specific questions for you to answer concerning your business. On this page you will also find suggestions for further reading on broader aspects of the subject of the assignment.

2. When tackling assignments this work pattern has proved successful:

   (a) Read up on the assignment and draft your own answer to the questions.
   (b) Discuss your answers, and any problems concerning the assignments with your prospective business partner(s), colleagues or some other knowledgeable individual such as an Enterprise Agency director, bank manager or accountant. If you are or plan to go on a small business or new enterprise training programme then your course tutor will also be able to help.

(c) Revise your own answers in the light of these discussions – and then let your colleagues and such other people as are involved, know your latest views on the assignment topic (you may need to go back and forth from steps b and c several times before you are entirely satisfied).

3. The contents of some assignments will suggest where and how to obtain the information needed to complete the assignment. However, don't expect to be told where to find all of the information about your business in these instructions. You will need to do some research yourself.

4. Example assignment completions taken from other business plans will also be presented to you in each assignment. These are presented only to give you a feel for the subject discussed. Your write-up of the assignment may need to be more or less elaborate, depending on your business.

5. The examples have been taken from actual business plans, but some have been changed in name and content, with some of the information purposely missing. Therefore do not copy a sample, however good it may sound; use it to help you to understand the purpose of the business plan assignment only.

6. Try to write up as much information as possible after reading each assignment. In this way you will know what remains to be researched (and do not wait until your information flows in perfect English before recording it).

7. Try to strike a balance between *qualitative* and *quantitative* statements in writing up your assignments. That is, try to back up as many of your statements as possible with numbers and documented sources of information. On the other hand, do not include numbers just because you have them; make sure that they really serve a purpose.

8. *Finally*, before attempting to write up your business plan make sure the answers to all the assignments are internally consistent – and if you have business partners make sure you are all in substantive agreement both at each stage and with the final outcome.

Believe it or not, the joint founders of one business fell out as they were making their presentation to a venture capital panel. Having divided up the workload of preparing the business plan, one had not told the other of some fairly major modifications to the product range, provoked as a result of completing the workbook assignments. (There was a happy ending but for a moment it was a close-run thing.)

Why Prepare a Business Plan?

Perhaps the most important step in launching any new venture or expanding an existing one is the construction of a business plan. Such a plan must include your goals for the enterprise, both short and long term; a description of the products or services you will offer and the market opportunities you have anticipated for them; finally, an explanation of the resources and means you will employ to achieve your goals in the face of likely competition.

Preparing a comprehensive business plan along these lines takes time and effort. In our experience at Cranfield on our new enterprise programmes, anything between 200 and 400 man hours is needed, depending on the nature of your business and how much data you have already gathered. Nevertheless, such an effort is essential if you are both to crystallise and focus your ideas, and test your resolve about entering or expanding your business. Once completed, your business plan will serve as a blueprint to follow which, like any map, improves the user's chances of reaching his destination.

There are a number of other important benefits you can anticipate arising from preparing a business plan. These include:

- This systematic approach to planning enables you to make your mistakes on paper, rather than in the market-place. One potential entrepreneur made the discovery while gathering data for his business plan that the local competitor he thought he was a one-man band was in fact the pilot operation for a proposed national chain of franchised outlets. This had a profound effect on his market entry strategy!

    Another entrepreneur found out that, at the price he proposed charging, he would never recover his overheads or break even. Indeed 'overheads' and 'break even' were themselves alien terms before he embarked on preparing a business plan. This naive perspective on costs is by no means unusual.

- Once completed, a business plan will make you feel more confident about your ability to set up and operate the venture. It may even compensate for lack of capital and experience, provided of course you have other factors in your favour, such as a sound idea and a sizeable market opportunity for your product or service.

- Your business plan will show how much money is needed, what it is needed for and when and for how long it is required.

As under-capitalisation and early cash flow problems are two important reasons why new business activities fail, it follows that those with a soundly prepared business plan can reduce these risks of failure. They can also experiment with a range of alternative viable strategies and so concentrate on options that make the most economic use of scarce financial resources.

It would be an exaggeration to say that your business plan is the passport to sources of finance. It will, however, help you to display your entrepreneurial flair and managerial talent to the full and to communicate your ideas to others in a way that will be easier for them to understand – and to appreciate the reasoning behind your ideas. These outside parties could be bankers, potential investors, partners or advisory agencies. Once they know what you are trying to do they will be better able to help you.

- Preparing a business plan will give you an insight into the planning process. It is this process itself that is important to the long-term health of a business, and not simply the plan that comes out of it. Businesses are dynamic, as are the commercial and competitive environments in which they operate. No one expects every event as recorded on a business plan to occur as predicted, but the understanding and knowledge created by the process of business planning will prepare the business for any changes that it may face, and so enable it to adjust quickly.

Despite these many valuable benefits, thousands of would-be entrepreneurs still attempt to start without a business plan. The most common among these are businesses that either appear to need little or no capital at the outset, or whose founders have funds of their own; in both cases it is believed unnecessary to expose the project to harsh financial appraisal.

The former hypothesis is usually based on the easily exploded myth that customers will all pay cash on the nail and suppliers will wait for months to be paid. In the meantime, the proprietor has the use of these funds to finance the business. Such model customers and suppliers are thinner on the ground than optimistic entrepreneurs think. In any event, two important market rules still apply: either the product or service on offer fails to sell like hot cakes and mountains of unpaid stocks build up, all of which eventually have to be financed; or it does sell like hot cakes and more financially robust entrepreneurs are attracted into the market. Without the staying power that adequate financing provides these new competitors will rapidly kill him off.

Those would-be entrepreneurs with funds of their own, or worse still borrowed from 'innocent' friends and relatives, tend to think that the time spent in preparing a business plan could be more usefully (and enjoyably) spent looking for premises, buying a new car, or installing a micro-computer. In short, anything that inhibits them from immediate action is viewed as time-wasting.

As most people's initial perception of their business venture is flawed in some important respect, it follows that jumping in at the deep end is risky – and unnecessarily so. Such flaws can often be discovered cheaply and in advance when preparing a business plan; they are always discovered in the market-place, invariably at a much higher and usually fatal cost.

What Financiers Look Out For

Successful entrepreneurs with a proven track record can have as many problems raising finance for their ventures as can the relative novice.

Bob Payton, who founded the Chicago Pizza Pie Factory in the late 1970s, related a story making exactly this point, to an enterprise programme at Cranfield:

'I now have a 10-year track record in the hospitality business. My company had a turnover of £10 million this year, and made a profit of £1 million. But the one constant problem I have had for the past 10 years has been raising finance to put my ideas into practice. Getting the £4.5 million for my latest venture, Stapleford Park, a country house hotel in Leicestershire will, by the time it opens in May, have taken three years. It has been as difficult and as gut-wrenching as trying to raise £35,000 for my first place, the Chicago Pizza Pie Factory.

Originally EMI had agreed to back my first venture. We'd shaken hands on the deal and I had ordered the ovens and gone off to the States to learn how to make pizza. When I came back I got a "Dear John" letter. They'd decided, on reflection, not to go ahead. I have that letter still, framed and hanging on the wall in my office. After a lot of trouble I finally raised the money elsewhere and went ahead. EMI were subsequently proved to be wrong.'

So if you need finance then, as well as the operational benefits of preparing a business plan, it is important to examine what financiers expect from you, if you are to succeed in raising those funds.

It is often said that there is no shortage of money for new and growing businesses – the only scarce commodities are good ideas and people with the ability to exploit them. From the potential entrepreneur's position this is often hard to believe. One major venture capital firm alone receives several thousand business plans a year. Only 500 or so are examined in any detail, less than 25 are pursued to the negotiating stage, and only six of those are invested in.

To a great extent the decision whether to proceed beyond an initial reading of the plan will depend on the quality of the business plan used in supporting the investment proposal. The business plan is the ticket of admission giving the entrepreneur his first and often only chance to impress prospective sources of finance with the quality of his proposal.

It follows from this that to have any chance at all of getting financial support, your business plan must be the best that can be written and it must be professionally packaged.

In our experience at Cranfield the plans that succeed meet all of the following requirements:

Evidence of market orientation and focus

David Stapleton, who took his company Pinneys from sales of £100,000 per annum in 1977 to over £30 million in 1987, learnt the lesson of concentration the hard way. He started out aiming to sell lamb, beef, venison and grouse, all products close at hand to his Scottish Borders home, to overseas markets. Full of enthusiasm he made a sales trip to the Far East, and went into the Peninsular Hotel in Hong Kong carrying, literally, a side of lamb on his back. But they didn't want to know about anything – except the smoked salmon. He made a loss of £14,000 on that trip, but he did discover what customers wanted. On the strength of that he raised £20,000 and bought out his smoked salmon supplier and his company now makes £1 million pa profit.

Entrepreneurs must demonstrate that they have recognised the needs of potential customers, rather than simply being infatuated with an innovative idea. Business plans that occupy more space with product descriptions and technical explanations, than with explaining how products will be sold and to whom, usually get cold-shouldered by financiers. They rightly suspect that these companies are more of an ego trip than an enterprise.

But market orientation is not in itself enough. Financiers want to sense that the entrepreneur knows the one or two things their business can do best – and that they are prepared to concentrate on exploiting these opportunities.

Two friends who eventually made it to an enterprise programme – and to founding a successful company – had great difficulty in getting backing at first. They were exceptionally talented designers and makers of clothes. They started out making ballgowns, wedding dresses, children's clothes – anything the market wanted. Only when they focused on designing and marketing clothes for the mother-to-be that allowed them still to feel fashionably dressed was it obvious they had a winning concept. That strategy built on their strength as designers, their experiences as former mothers-to-be, and exploited a clear market opportunity neglected at that time by the main player in the market-place – Mothercare.

Evidence of customer acceptance

Financiers like to know that the product or service a new venture will sell is being used, even if only on a trial or demonstration basis.

The founder of Solicitec, a company selling software to solicitors to enable them to process relatively standard documents such as wills and house conveyancing, had little trouble getting support for his business once his product had been tried and approved by a leading building society for their panel of solicitors.

If you are only at the prototype stage then, as well as having to assess your chances of succeeding with technology, financiers have no immediate indication that, once made, your product will appeal to the market. Under these circumstances you have to show that the 'problem' your innovation seeks to solve is a substantial one that a large number of people will pay for.

One young inventor at the Royal College of Art came up with a revolutionary toilet system design, that as well as being extremely thin, used 30 per cent less water per flush and had half the number of moving parts of a conventional product, all for no increase in price. Although he had only drawings to show, it was clear that with domestic metered water for all households on the immediate horizon, and a UK market for half a million new units per annum, a sizeable acceptance was reasonably certain.

As well as evidence of customer acceptance, entrepreneurs need to demonstrate that they know how and to whom their product or service must be sold, and that they have a financially viable means of doing so.

Proprietary position

Exclusive rights to a product through patents, copyright, trademark protection or a licence helps to reduce the apparent riskiness of a venture in the financier's eyes, as these can limit competition – for a while at least.

One participant on a Cranfield enterprise programme held patents on a revolutionary folding bicycle he had designed at college. While no financial institution was prepared to back him in manufacturing the bicycle, funds were readily available to enable him to make production prototypes and then license manufacture to established bicycle makers throughout the world.

However well protected legally a product is, it is marketability and marketing know-how generally that outweigh 'patentability' in the success equation. A salutary observation made by an American Professor of Entrepreneurship revealed that less than 0.5 per cent of the best ideas contained in the US *Patent Gazette* in the last five years have returned a dime to the inventors.

Financiers' needs

Anyone lending money to or investing in a venture will expect the entrepreneur to have given some thought to his needs, and to have explained how they can be accommodated in the business plan.

Bankers, and indeed any other sources of debt capital, are looking for asset security to back their loan and the near certainty of getting their money back. They will also charge an interest rate which reflects current market conditions and their view of the risk level of the proposal. Depending on the nature of the business in question and the purpose for which the money is being used, bankers will take a five- to fifteen-year view.

As with a mortgage repayment, bankers will usually expect a business to start repaying both the loan and the interest on a monthly or quarterly basis immediately the loan has been granted. In some cases a capital 'holiday' for up to two years can be negotiated, but in the early stage of any loan the interest charges make up the lion's share of payments.

Bankers hope the business will succeed so that they can lend more money in the future and provide more banking services such as insurance, tax advice etc to a loyal customer.

It follows from this appreciation of a lender's needs that they are less interested in rapid growth and the consequent capital gain than they are in a steady stream of earnings almost from the outset.

As most new or fast growing businesses generally do not make immediate profits, money for such enterprises must come from elsewhere. Risk or equity capital, as other types of funds are called, comes from venture capital houses, as well as being put in by founders, their families and friends.

Because the inherent risks involved in investing in new and young ventures are greater than for investing in established companies, venture capital fund managers have to offer their investors the chance of larger overall returns. To do that, fund managers must not only keep failures to a minimum; they have to pick some big winners too – ventures with annual compound growth rates above 50 per cent – to offset the inevitable mediocre performers.

Debbie Moore's Pineapple dance studios was one such company. Introduced to the Unlisted Securities Market (USM) in 1982 by its venture capital providers, its shares quickly went to an 85 per cent premium. Profits rose by 50 per cent in 1983, as forecast, and the company raised a further £1.5 million via a rights issue. Ms Moore was even given the coveted Businesswoman of the Year award.

But this time the moneymen were not so fortunate. In 1985 aerobics began to lose its popular appeal as health experts cast doubts on its efficacy. By May the company was in a nosedive, showing half-year losses of £197,000. In the latter half of 1985 Peter Bain, a new boardroom recruit, evolved a strategy to turn the company into a marketing services group. After several acquisitions and a total change of direction, Pineapple reported profits of £1.25 million in 1986.

But the dance studios clearly couldn't be made to work. 'It soon became obvious,' to quote Moore, 'that it was difficult to deliver the kind of money the City wanted out of dance.' Ms Moore resigned from the Pineapple Group in December 1987, taking the loss-making dance studios with her for a nominal sum, leaving the rest of the Group to pursue its new strategy.

Typically, a fund manager would expect from any 10 investments: one star, seven also-rans, and two flops. It is important to remember that despite this outcome, venture capital fund managers are only looking for winners, so unless you are projecting high capital growth, the chances of getting venture capital are against you.

Not only are venture capitalists looking for winners, they are also looking for a substantial shareholding in your business. There are no simple rules for what constitutes a fair split, but *Venture Capital Report*, a UK monthly publication of investment opportunities, suggests the following starting point:

For the idea: 33%
For the management: 33%
For the money: 34%

It all comes down to how much you need the money, how risky the venture is, how much money could be made – and your skills as a negotiator. However, it is salutory to remember that 100 per cent of nothing is still nothing. So all parties to the deal have to be satisfied if it is to succeed.

Venture capital firms may also want to put a non-executive director on the board of your company to look after their interests. You will have at your disposal a talented financial brain so be prepared to make use of him, as his services won't be free – you'll either pay up front in the fee for raising the capital, or you'll pay an annual management charge.

As fast-growing companies typically have no cash available to pay dividends, investors can only profit by selling their holdings. With this in mind the venture capitalist needs to have an exit route such as the Stock Exchange or a potential corporate buyer in view at the outset.

Unlike many entrepreneurs (and some lending bankers) who see their ventures as life-long commitments to success and growth, venture capitalists have a relatively short time horizon. Typically, they are looking to liquidate small company investments within three to seven years, allowing them to pay out individual investors and to have funds available for tomorrow's winners.

So, to be successful your business must be targeted at the needs of these two sources of finance, and in particular at the balance between the two. Lending bankers ideally look for a ratio of £1 of debt to £1 of equity capital, but have been known to go up to £4–£5. Venture capital providers will almost always encourage entrepreneurs to take on new debt capital to match the level of equity funding.

If you plan to raise money from friends and relatives their needs must also be taken into account in your business plan. Their funds can be in the form of debt or equity, but they may also seek some management role for themselves. Unless they have an important contribution to make, by virtue of being an accountant or marketing expert or respected public figure, for example, it is always best to confine their role to that of a shareholder. In that capacity they can 'give' you advice or pass on their contacts and so enhance the worth of their (and your) shareholding, but they won't hold down a post that would be better filled by someone else. Alternatively, make them non-executive directors, which may flatter them and can't harm your business. Clearly, you must use common-sense in this area.

One final point on the needs of financial institutions: they will expect your business plan to include a description of how performance will be monitored and controlled.

One budding entrepreneur blew an otherwise impeccable performance at a bankers' panel, by replying when asked how he would control his venture: 'I'm only concerned with raising finance and getting my business started at the moment – once that's over I'll think about "bean counting".'

He had clearly forgotten who owned the beans!

Believable forecasts

Entrepreneurs are naturally ebullient when explaining the future prospects for their businesses. They frequently believe that 'the sky's the limit' when it comes to growth, and money (or rather the lack of it) is the only thing that stands between them and their success.

It is true that if you are looking for venture capital, then the providers are also looking for rapid growth. However, it's as well to remember that financiers are dealing with thousands of investment proposals each year, and already have money tied up in hundreds of business sectors. It follows, therefore, that they already have a perception of what the accepted financial results and marketing approaches currently are, for any sector. Any new company's business plan showing projections that are outside the ranges perceived as acceptable within an industry will raise questions in the investor's mind.

Make your growth forecasts believable; support them with hard facts where possible. If they are on the low side, then approach the more cautious lending banker, rather than venture capitalists. The former often see a modest forecast as a virtue, lending credibility to the business proposal as a whole.

Phase 1
History and Position to Date

Assignment 1
Introduction to Your Business

In this first assignment you should introduce your business idea to the future readers of your business plan. Explain something of how you arrived at your business idea, why you think people have a need for your product or service, and what your goals and aspirations for the business are. If your business needs financing you could give some preliminary idea of how much you may need and what you intend to do with those funds. Remember, all these ideas are likely to be significantly modified later on – some more than others – but you need to have some idea at the outset of where you are going if you are to have any chance at all of getting there.

> Michael Golder, who founded Kennedy Brookes (KB), the first of the new wave of publicly quoted catering companies, in 1980 defined his objectives in this way: 'From the start I wanted this to be a big company. I never, for example, wanted to run my own restaurant. Therefore we laid our emphasis on professional management whose skills lay in the field of raising finance and takeovers.'
>
> Golder began with a single hamburger joint in the Old Brompton Road – Brookes – now transformed into Hilaire. His first year's turnover was a quarter of a million. By 1987 it was over £65 million. Shares, which were placed at 36p, rose rapidly to 417p and so formed the mechanism by which KB's goals and aspirations could be achieved.
>
> From the outset Golder embarked on a series of takeovers and new developments in rapid succession: Fads (1980); Mario & Franco (1981); Genevieve (a group of restaurants, including Lockets, formerly belonging to Joseph Berkmann) (1982); Maxim's de Paris (1983); Wheeler's (1983); Trocadero Restaurants (1984); London Pavilion (1984); Cafés des Amis and Amis du Vin (1984); The Bear Group (1985); Crusts (1986); Christopher & Co Ltd (a very pukka old wine merchant with the Royal warrant) (1987); Heritage Hotels (11 hotels, including the Imperial at Blackpool, for which KB paid £35 million) (1987); Onslow Court (1987); and Black & Edgington (suppliers of marquees etc, an astute purchase that 'will enable our outside catering to offer a more integrated service than our competitors') (1987).

It may be useful to organise your information in this section using the pyramid of goals on page 26 as a framework.

The pyramid of goals

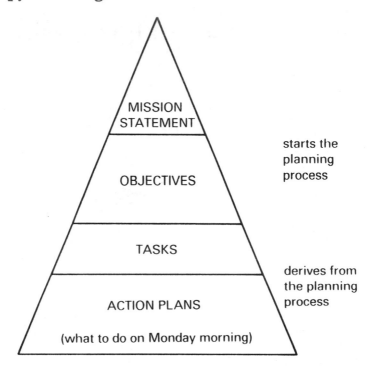

Note: Mission and objectives are 'what' statements;
tasks and action plans are 'how to' statements.

To take mission statements and objectives first, as they are inevitably intertwined, these are direction statements, intended to focus your attention on essentials, to encapsulate your specific competence(s), in relation to the markets/customers you plan to serve.

First, the mission should be narrow enough to give direction and guidance to everyone in the business. This concentration is the key to business success because it is only by focusing on specific needs that a small business can differentiate itself from its larger competitors. Nothing kills off a new business faster than trying to do too many different things at the outset.

Second, the mission should open up a large enough market to allow the business to grow and realise its potential.

Interestingly enough, one of the highest incidences of failure in small business is in the building trade. The very nature of this field seems to mitigate against being able to concentrate on any specific type of work, or on customer need. One successful new small builder defined his mission in the following sentence. 'We will concentrate on domestic house repair and renovation work, and as well as doing a good job we will meet the customers' two key needs: a quotation that is accurate, and starting and completion dates that are met.' When told this mission, most small builders laugh. They say it cannot be done, but then most go broke.

Ultimately, there has to be something unique about your business idea or yourself that makes people want to buy from you. That uniqueness may be confined to the fact that you are the only photocopying shop in the area, but that is enough to make you stand out (provided, of course, that the area has potential customers).

Also, within the objectives you need some idea of how big you want the business to be. Your share of the market, in other words. It certainly is not easy to forecast sales, especially before you have even started trading, but if you do not set a goal at the start and instead just wait to see how things develop, then one of two problems will occur. Either you will not sell enough to cover your fixed costs and so lose money and perhaps go out of business, or you will sell too much and run out of cash, in other words, overtrade.

Obviously, before you can set a market share and sales objective you need to know the size of your market. We shall consider how to find that out in later assignments.

The 'size' you want your business to be is more a matter of judgement than forecast – a judgement tempered by the resources you have available to achieve those objectives and, of course, some idea of what is reasonable and achievable and what is not. You will find the range of discretion over a size objective seriously constrained by the financial resources at your disposal – or realistically available from investors and lenders – and the scope of the market opportunity.

It will be useful to set near-term objectives covering the next 18 months or so, and a longer-term objective covering up to five or so years on.

In summary, the mission statement should explain what business you are in or plan to enter. It should include some or all of the following:

- Market/customer needs – who are we 'satisfying'?
- With what product/service will we meet that need?
- What are our capabilities, both particular skills and knowledge, and resources?
- What market opportunities are there for our product or service, and what threats are there from competitors (and others)?
- What do we enjoy doing most?

- What do we want to achieve, both now and in the future?

Above all, mission statements must be realistic, achievable – and brief.

> Blooming Marvellous is a company formed by two young mothers who, while attending an enterprise programme, developed the following mission statement:
>
> 'Arising out of our experiences, we intend to design, make and market a range of clothes for mothers-to-be that will make them feel they can still be fashionably dressed. We aim to serve a niche missed out by Mothercare, Marks & Spencer etc, and so become a significant force in the mail order fashion for the mothers-to-be market. We are aiming for a 5 per cent share of this market in the south-east, and a 25 per cent return on assets employed within three years of starting up. We believe we will need about £25,000 start-up capital to finance stock, a mail order catalogue and an advertising campaign.'

Blooming Marvellous's co-founder turned this mission statement, together with their principal objectives, into a key tasks and action plan. This plan consists of 'how to' statements to achieve specific objectives and goals.

Objective:

- Achieve 5 per cent market share in south-east of UK, and a 25 per cent return on assets employed.

Tasks:

- Identify mailing lists and promotion media within three months.
- Design 12 items of fashion clothes within six months.
- Produce mail order catalogue within nine months.
- Locate packaging and distributor organisations within six months.

Action plan:

Monday morning:

- Start design on one product.
- Write for mailing list details.
- Look up trade directories for distributors.

It would also be useful at this stage to explain how you arrived at your business idea, what makes you believe it will succeed, and why you want to go ahead with it now.

McIntosh's business, Safariquip, equips safaris, or anyone else planning long, overland travel. The corporate and institutional market – involving expeditions and surveys for oil or minerals, or other projects in the Third World – is just beginning to open up too.

The idea was born out of the difficulties McIntosh experienced when he went exploring Africa by Land Rover and climbing mountains there in the 1970s. It took him two years to prepare for the trip. There was no single source of help, advice or supplies. This gave him the first inkling that there might be a market. Was it, he asked himself, the same for all similar overland travellers, whether going on safari, travelling for fun, mounting geographical expeditions or even prospecting for minerals?

Experience, he was to discover, showed that anyone travelling long distances over rough terrain and living in the bush for long periods while doing so, needed much the same sort of equipment and advice. Much of the equipment, though basic, is special enough to be scattered among many different sources and difficult to obtain in total because of the problems involved in tracking down all the individual sources.

His other discoveries during his African safari included the disconcerting fact that roofracks on vehicles destroy the points at which they are anchored during the course of 21,000 miles of driving over rough ground. The solution as he saw it was to find better-designed and more easily stowable items in the first place, as well as redesigning stowage facilities inside the vehicle. He rebuilt his vehicle from the chassis up during two years in South Africa, funding his work by taking a job as a middle manager in a mining company. He then, over a further two-year period, returned home, learning yet more about travelling and rough driving.

It was redundancy, after a variety of jobs, that pushed him finally into making his move. 'I decided to market my skills as a traveller. Many people need to know how to do it. I put an ad in *The Traveller* magazine, offering equipment and advice and started to pick up business very gradually.'

Worksheet for Assignment 1: Business purpose and aims

1. Explain how you arrived at your business idea.
2. What makes you believe it will succeed?
3. Write a mission statement linking your product or service to the customer needs it is aimed at.
4. What are your principal objectives?

   (a) Short term
   (b) Long term

5. List your tasks and action plans as you see them at present.
6. How much money do you think will be needed to get your business started? Provide a short 'shopping list' of major expenses.

Suggested further reading
Managing for Results, Peter Drucker, Pan Books, 1967.

Assignment 2
A Description of Your Business

The two essential ingredients for success in any new venture are a good business idea and the right people to turn that idea into a business. Your business plan must therefore include not only a description of what your purpose or mission is, but give full details of you and your prospective partners' experience and 'suitability' for this venture.

You also need to explain the name of your business, why you chose it, and under what legal form you propose to trade. If your business has been trading for some time, you should give a brief description of achievements to date and a summary of financial results. Full accounts can be included in an appendix to your business plan. Let's look at each in turn:

You and your team

The right stuff

To launch a new venture successfully, you have to be the right sort of person, your business idea must be right for the market, and your timing must be spot on. The world of business failures is full of products that are ahead of their time.

The entrepreneur is frequently seen as someone who is always bursting with new ideas, is highly enthusiastic, hyperactive and insatiably curious. But the more you try to create a picture of the typical entrepreneur, the more elusive he becomes.

Peter Drucker, the international business guru, captured the problem clearly with this description:

'Some are eccentrics, others painfully correct conformists; some are fat and some are lean; some are worriers, some relaxed; some drink quite heavily, others are total abstainers; some are men of great charm and warmth, some have no more personality than a frozen mackerel.'

Having said that, there are certain characteristics which successful newcomers to business do have in common, and you should emphasise these in respect to yourself in the business plan.

Self-confident all-rounders

Entrepreneurs are rarely geniuses. There are nearly always people in their business who have more competence, in one field, than they could ever aspire to. But they have a wide range of ability and a willingness to turn their hands to anything that has to be done to make the venture succeed. They can usually make the product, market it and count the money, but above all they have self-confidence that lets them move comfortably through uncharted waters.

> Paul Smith, who left school at 15, launched his clothing business in 1974 and within a decade had opened three shops in London, one of which is in Covent Garden, and a further one in Tokyo. Turnover is now above £2 million pa.
>
> Explaining his success he states: 'It's not that I'm a particularly brilliant designer or businessman, but I can run a business and I can design. There are so many excellent designers or excellent business people but so often the designers can't run the business and businessmen do not have the right product.'
>
> Bob Payton, founder of the Chicago Pizza Pie Factory, explained how his first venture got started. 'I had no catering experience, but I've got a nose for what's going on. I flew to Chicago, located the best pizza chef and spent two weeks learning the business. I made dough, waited at tables and washed dishes – and then I set out to raise £25,000 to start up.'

The ability to bounce back

Rising from the ashes of former disasters is also a common feature of many successful entrepreneurs.

> Henry Ford had been bankrupted twice before founding the Ford Motor Corporation with a loan of $28,000 in his fortieth year.
>
> In 1982, Timothy Waterstone, founder of one of the fastest growing book chains in the West, was fired from W H Smith's US operation in the most bloodcurdling circumstances. He took the first plane back and spent two months wondering what to do.
>
> Until this time Waterstone's career path had been smooth and unmeteoric. After Cambridge he did a spell in the family tea-broking business in Cochin, followed by 10 years as a marketing manager for Allied Breweries. Books had always been his obsession, so he went to work for W H Smith. He was quickly sent to New York, where he remained for four years. His wife was in the UK for long periods, so he spent his spare time wandering around Manhattan bookshops. Brilliant places: lively and consumer-led with huge stock, accessible staff and long opening hours. He felt there was a gap for similar bookselling in Britain, but at the time did nothing about it.

A trip to the dole office acted as a catalyst. It was the most horrific experience of his life. Not waiting for his turn, he rushed out and sat in the car. Instead of trying to get a new job, he formulated the Waterstone's concept. High street banks turned him down. He then went to a finance house and struck lucky. He pledged his house, £6000 savings, £10,000 borrowed from his father-in-law, and the rest was raised through the Government's loan guarantee scheme.

Three months later, the first Waterstone's opened. Based on a simple store plan an art student sketched out for £25, he filled the shops with the type of books that appeal to book lovers, not best-seller buyers. Midnight hours, Sunday trading (where possible) and bonus schemes for staff led to dazzling sales and the company now employs 500 people in 40 branches, has a turnover of £35 million a year, and is all set for a Stock Exchange flotation.

Innovative skills

Almost by definition, entrepreneurs are innovators who either tackle the unknown, or do old things in new ways. It is this inventive streak that allows them to carve out a new niche, often invisible to others.

Trees Unlimited, which has recently passed the £1 million sales mark, was formed three years ago from a nucleus of former managers of Porth Textiles, once Britain's largest manufacturer of decorations, garlands and plastic trees. Roger Freebody, Trees Unlimited's managing director, saw the writing on the wall before Porth collapsed with debts of £8 million, putting 364 people out of work in the Rhondda Valley.

Freebody and his colleagues saw the keys to survival as being able to escape from old fashioned manufacturing traditions and being able to innovate and try new marketing approaches. Trees Unlimited has introduced a whole range of coloured trees from brown to pink, thus bucking the tradition that said Christmas trees *had* to be green. It has also introduced a new marketing concept of matching trees and their decorations with home decors. Now even the Queen's florist in Berkeley Square is one of their customers.

Valerie Askew, the founder of one of Britain's oldest and most respected model agencies, set her business up in 1966 with just £150 capital. In her first year she did £600 worth of business. By 1987 she employed 19 people in Britain and 38 in Japan. Her turnover was over £5 million. Describing her success Askew stated, 'It is hard work. To remain a top agency you have always got to be finding new faces and coming up with new ideas' – innovation is the key.

Results oriented

Successful people set themselves goals and get pleasure out of trying to achieve them. Once a goal has been reached, they have to get the next target in view as quickly as possible. This restlessness is very characteristic. Sir James Goldsmith is a classic example, moving the base of his business empire from the UK to France, then the USA – and finally into pure cash, ahead of the 1987 stock market crash.

James Gulliver, who built the Argyll group up to the fourth largest food retailer in the UK in around a decade, also exhibited this restless streak when he resigned in November 1987, still only in his fifties, to make a third 'fresh' start in his career.

Professional risk-taker

The high failure rate shows that small businesses are faced with many dangers. An essential characteristic of someone starting a business is a willingness to make decisions and to take risks. This does not mean gambling on hunches. It means carefully calculating the odds and deciding which risks to take and when to take them.

Having total commitment

You will need complete faith in your idea. How else will you convince all the doubters you are bound to meet that it is a worthwhile venture? You will also need singlemindedness, energy and a lot of hard work to get things started; working 18-hour days is not uncommon. This can put a strain on other relationships, particularly within your family, so they too have to become involved and committed if you are to succeed.

> Technophone, founded in 1984 by Nils Mortensson, grew its turnover from zero to an expected £20 million in 1988, with profit forecast at more than £3 million.
>
> Mortensson came up with the idea of a shirt-pocket sized cellphone in 1972. 'Nobody then believed it could be done that small and they still didn't believe me 10 years later. We proved them wrong and now our competitors have had to eat their words and buy in from us.'
>
> Marketed as the Excell Phone, Mortensson's product is now made by a workforce of 600 at his Surrey factory. It took him 12 months to raise the £5.5 million needed to fund the venture and he had to take his business plan to 11 city investors before he got the right deal.

All too often budding entrepreneurs believe themselves to be the right sort of person to set up a business. Unfortunately, the capacity for self-deception is enormous. When a random sample of male adults were asked recently to rank themselves on leadership ability, 70 per cent rated themselves in the top 25 per cent; only 2 per cent felt they were below average as leaders. In an area in which self-deception ought to be difficult, 60 per cent said they were well above average in athletic ability and only 6 per cent said they were below.

A common mistake made in assessing entrepreneurial talent is to assume that success in big business management will automatically guarantee success in a small business.

Lore Hap, who took her company Vector Graphics from a $6000 investment to a £25-million company in five years, when asked if a grooming at IBM would have helped her on her way replied:

'We are one of the pioneers of the micro-computer explosion. The buying, as well as the selling process in this industry is different from what it had been before for computers. Buyers were much less sophisticated; they really didn't know what they wanted. So I think the principles that I may have learned at IBM, DEC, or any other computer company would probably not have served me well at all. We are dealing with a totally new element.'

Building the team

Not surprisingly, an investor's ideal proposal includes an experienced and balanced management team, who have all worked together for a number of years. That will ensure management in depth, thus providing cover for everything from illness to expansion, and guaranteeing some stability during the turbulent early years. For this reason management buy-outs are a firm favourite.

At the other end of the scale is the lone inventor whose management skills may be in doubt, and who is anyway fully stretched getting his product from the drawing board to the production line. This type of proposal is unlikely to attract much investment capital. It has obvious risks beyond those every company expects to experience in the market-place. In any case, without a management team in place the business is ill prepared for the rapid growth required to service an investor's funds.

In practice, most business proposals lie somewhere between these extremes. Your business plan should explain clearly what the ideal composition of key managers should be for your business; who you have identified, or recruited so far; and last but certainly not least, how you will motivate them to remain with you and perform well for at least the first few all important years.

F International, set up by a group of technologically skilled women whose family ties made it impossible for them to work standard office hours, nearly floundered when six full-time staff left in 1982 to form their own business. They took with them many F International customers, as well as the business concept. F International's profits for the year up to this defection were £450,000. For the year 1982–83 profits slumped to £124,000 and it wasn't until 1984–85 that profits partially recovered to £340,000.

Certainly investors will look for reassurance in this respect and will expect to see some reference to the steps you will take to encourage loyalty.

Your business name

The main consideration in choosing a business name is its commercial usefulness. It is unlikely, for example, that Boris Karloff would have had such a successful career as a horror movie star using his own name, William Pratt.

Emma Bridgewater set up her business in 1984, 18 months after completing an English degree at Bedford College, London. At first she wasn't sure what business to start but her boyfriend at the time, with whom she lived in Brixton, wanted to set up a craft studio to teach students how to slip-cast (an ancient method of making pottery with liquid clay poured into a mould). Emma visited factories in Stoke-on-Trent and discovered a number of people with this skill. 'Their mug shapes were revolting, though. So I drew my own. I found, doing so, that all my frustration evaporated just like that. Suddenly I knew what I wanted to do.'

The next few months were spent driving up and down the motorway in her Mini Metro, staying in travelling salesmen's hotels. She equipped herself with sponges and colours so that she could apply her designs to her mugs in the factories.

'At first the people in Stoke thought I was mad and were sceptical but helpful.' However, in February 1985 she won her first order, worth £600, from the General Trading Company, and in April she joined a lot of 'hysterical stall-holders with lavender bags' at a trade fair in Kensington: Brixton Spongeware was launched. She has since changed the name: "I was fed up with jokes about reggae music and sweet potatoes. The name Bridgewater is far more appropriate. It sounds like an old established industry. People often imagine it's a family business that has been going for years. That's exactly the mood I want to create.'

Just over two years later she has a file full of orders from top department stores in London and New York. Cheap imitators have already started copying her designs.

You must select a name that will let people know as much about your business, its products and services as possible. Since 26 February 1982, when the provisions of the Companies Act 1981 came into effect, there have been some new rules that could influence your choice of name.

First, anyone wanting to use a 'controlled' name will have to get permission. There are some 80 or 90 controlled names that include words such as 'International', 'Bank' and 'Royal'. This is simply to prevent a business implying that it is something that it is not.

Second, all businesses that intend to trade under names other than those of their owner(s) must state who does own the business and how the owner can be contacted. So if you are a sole trader or partnership and you only use surnames with or without forenames or initials, you are not affected. Companies are also not affected if they simply use their full corporate name.

A Guidance Note entitled 'Control of Business Names' is available from the Department of Trade and Industry.

If any name other than the 'true' name is to be used, then you must disclose the name of the owner(s) and an address in the UK to which business documents can be sent. This information has to be shown on all business letters, orders for goods and services, invoices and receipts, and statements and demands for business debts. Also, a copy has to be displayed prominently on all business premises. The purpose of the Act is simply to make it easier to 'see' who you are doing business with.

If you are setting up as a limited company you will have to submit your choice of names to the Companies Registration Office along with the other documents required for registration. It will be accepted unless there is another company with that name on the register or the Registrar considers the name to be obscene, offensive or illegal.

Contact:

Department of Trade and Industry
1 Victoria Street, London SW1H 0ET
01-215 7877

Companies Registration Office
Crown Way, Maindy, Cardiff CF4 3HZ
0222 388588

Deciding the legal form of your business

Before you start trading you will need to consider what legal form your business will take. There are four main forms that a business can take and the one you choose will depend on a number of factors: commercial needs, financial risk and your tax position.

Each of these forms is explained briefly below, together with the procedure to follow on setting them up.

Sole trader

The vast majority of new businesses set up each year in the UK choose to do so as sole traders. It has the merit of being relatively formality free and, unless you intend to register for VAT, there are no rules about the records you have to keep. There is no requirement for your accounts to be audited, or for financial information on your business to be filed at Companies House.

As a sole trader there is no legal distinction between you and your business – your business is one of your assets, just as your house or car is.

It follows from this that if your business should fail your creditors have a right not only to the assets of the business, but also to your personal assets, subject only to the provisions of the Bankruptcy Acts (these allow you to keep only a few absolutely basic essentials for yourself and family).

It is possible to avoid the worst of these consequences by ensuring that your private assets are the legal property of your spouse, against whom your creditors have no claim. (You must be solvent when the transfer is made, and that transfer must have been made at least two years prior to your business running into trouble.) However, to be effective such a transfer must be absolute and you can have no say in how your spouse chooses to dispose of his or her new found wealth!

The capital to get the business going must come from you – or from loans. There is no access to equity capital, which has the attraction of being risk-free. In return for these drawbacks you can have the pleasure of being your own boss immediately, subject only to declaring your profits on your tax return. (In practice you would be wise to take professional advice before doing so.)

Partnerships

Partnerships are effectively collections of sole traders and, as such, share the legal problems attached to personal liability. There are very few restrictions to setting up in business with another person (or persons) in partnership, and several definite advantages. By pooling resources you may have more capital; you will be bringing, hopefully, several sets of skills to the business; and if you are ill the business can still carry on.

There are two serious drawbacks that merit particular attention. First, if your partner makes a business mistake, perhaps by signing a disastrous contract, without your knowledge or consent, every member of the partnership must shoulder the consequences. Under these circumstances your personal assets could be taken to pay the creditors even though the mistake was no fault of your own.

Second, if your partner goes bankrupt in his personal capacity, for whatever reason, his share of the partnership can be seized by his creditors. As a private individual you are not liable for his private debts, but having to buy him out of the partnership at short notice could put you and the business in financial jeopardy. Even death may not release you from partnership obligations and in some circumstances your estate can remain liable. Unless you take 'public' leave of your partnership by notifying your business contacts, and advertising your retirement in *The London Gazette*, you will remain liable indefinitely.

The legal regulations governing this field are set out in the Partnership Act 1890, which in essence assumes that competent businessmen should know what they are doing. The Act merely provides a framework of agreement which applies 'in the absence of agreement to the contrary'. It follows from this that many partnerships are entered into without legal formalities – and sometimes without the parties themselves being aware that they have entered a partnership!

The main provisions of the Partnership Act state:

- All partners contribute capital equally.
- All partners share profits and losses equally.
- No partner shall have interest paid on his capital.
- No partner shall be paid a salary.
- All partners have an equal say in the management of the business.

It is unlikely that all these provisions will suit you so you would be well advised to get a 'partnership agreement' drawn up in writing by a solicitor, at the outset of your venture.

One possibility that can reduce the more painful consequences of entering a partnership as a 'sleeping partner' is to have your involvement registered as a limited partnership. It means you (or your partner) can play no active part in running the business, but your risks are limited to the capital that you put in.

Unless you are a member of certain professions (eg, law, accountancy etc) you are restricted to a maximum of 20 partners in any partnership.

Co-operative

A co-operative is an enterprise owned and controlled by the people working in it. Once in danger of becoming extinct, the workers' co-operative is enjoying something of a comeback, and there are over 1500 operating in the UK. They are growing at the rate of 20 per cent per annum.

Co-operatives are governed by the Industrial and Provident Societies Act 1965, whose main provisions state:

- Each member of the co-operative has equal control through the principle of 'one person one vote'.
- Membership must be open to anyone who satisfies the stipulated qualifications.
- Profits can be retained in the business or distributed in proportion to members' involvement, eg hours worked.
- Members must benefit primarily from their participation in the business.
- Interest on loan or share capital is limited in some specific way, even if the profits are high enough to allow a greater payment.

It is certainly not a legal structure designed to give entrepreneurs control of their own destiny and maximum profits. However, if this is to be your chosen legal form you can pay £50 to register with the Chief Registrar of Friendly Societies, and must have at least seven members at the outset. They do not all have to be full-time workers at first. Like a limited company, a registered co-operative has limited liability (see under Limited liability companies) for its members and must file annual accounts, but there is no charge for this. Not all co-operatives bother to register as it isn't mandatory, in which case they are treated in law as a partnership with unlimited liability.

Limited liability companies

In the UK, before the 1985 Companies Act, it was necessary to have an Act of Parliament or a Royal Charter in order to set up a company. Now, out of the 2.5 million businesses trading in the UK, over 1 million are limited companies. As the name suggests, in this form of business your liability is limited to the amount you contribute by way of share capital.

A limited company has a legal identity of its own, separate from the people who own or run it. This means that, in the event of failure, creditors' claims are restricted to the assets of the company. The shareholders of the business are not liable as individuals for the business debts beyond the paid-up value of their shares. This applies even if the shareholders are working directors, unless of course the company has been trading fraudulently. (In practice, the ability to limit liability is severely restricted these days as most lenders, including the banks, often insist on personal guarantees from the directors.)

Other advantages include the freedom to raise capital by selling shares.

Disadvantages include the legal requirement for the company's accounts to be audited by a chartered or certified accountant. This is unlikely to cost much less than £500 per annum, and is more likely to run to four figures than three.

A limited company can be formed by two shareholders, one of whom must be a director. A company secretary must also be appointed, who can be a shareholder, director, or an outside person such as an accountant or lawyer.

The company can be bought 'off the shelf' from a registration agent, then adapted to suit your own purposes. This will involve changing the name, shareholders and articles of association, and will cost about £250 and take a couple of weeks to arrange. Alternatively, you can form your own company, using your solicitor or accountant. This will cost around £500 and take six to eight weeks.

The behaviour of companies and their directors is governed by the various Companies Acts that have come into effect since 1844.

Further information
Board of Inland Revenue
Press Office, Somerset House, Strand, London WC2R 1LB

Institute of Chartered Accountants in England and Wales
PO Box 433, Chartered Accountants Hall, Moorgate Place,
London EC2P 2BJ
01-628 7070

In Ireland: 11 Donegall Square, Belfast BT1 5JE
0232 221600

In Scotland: 27 Queen Street, Edinburgh EH2 1LA
031-225 5673

Chief Registrar of Friendly Societies
17 North Audley Street, London W1Y 2AP
01-629 7001

Co-operative Development Agency
21 Panton Street, London SW1Y 4DR
01-839 2988

The Law Society
113 Chancery Lane, London WC2A 1PL
01-242 1222

The Registrar of Companies
Companies House, Crown Way, Maindy, Cardiff CF4 3VZ
0222 388588

Past achievements

If your business has already been trading for some time, your business
plan should include a summary of past results and achievements.
Annual reports, audited accounts etc, if voluminous, can be included in
an appendix, and referred to in this section of your business plan.
Otherwise they can be shown in detail. You should emphasise what you
have learnt so far that convinces you your strategies are soundly based.

Windancer (the situation in the spring of 1982)

Tim Langley Airwheels was set up in 1978 as a limited company with an
initial share capital of £20,000. The company's principal product is the
Windancer, a unique land yacht using Langley's own invention, the air
wheel.
 The air wheel is a light, chunky, bouncy wheel whose tyre is treadless.

41

It exhibits a number of useful properties which make it ideal for movement across both soft and rough ground.

The wheel was originally conceived with the idea of boat launching in mind. This has not proved a commercially viable proposition, so far at least. A number of reasons are involved: many launching sites are concreted because of known difficulties; launching trailers should ideally double as car trailers; air wheels have no tread etc.

Commercial development has concentrated on using the air wheel, which now enjoys patent protection, as the unique element on the Windancer – a superior land/sand yacht.

This development took 18 months and the sales and profit history for Windancer are set out below.

Year	Sales (units)	Profit (loss)
1979	10	(12,000)
1980	30	(8,000)
1981	70	350
1982 (1st quarter)	25	3,000 budget

The market, though difficult to quantify, appears to have grown from virtually zero in 1978 to some 14,000 units per annum now (1982). It is much greater on the Continent, especially in France.

Distributor margins are around 50 per cent normally. We have pitched our price and margins high for two reasons. It makes more profit for our distributors and so makes them keen to sell Windancer; it emphasises our 'uniqueness' and product superiority in the market-place.

Our main competitor, the Landsailer, is both lower in quality and price, and we are confident sales can rise rapidly to 500 units per annum, with additional investment in manufacturing processes.

Worksheet for Assignment 2: A description of your business

1. What is your business name and why have you chosen it?
2. What experience and skills do you have that are particularly relevant to this venture?
3. Who else will be working with you and what relevant experience and skills do they have?
4. Draw an organisation chart showing who is responsible for which functions.
5. What people (or skill) gaps are there in the organisation you need to run your business? How do you plan to fill them?
6. How will you ensure that your key staff are motivated and loyal during the start-up period?
7. What professional advisers (accountant, lawyer, patent agent etc)

have you used, or do you plan to use?
8. Under what legal form will you trade and why?
9. If your business is already trading, give a brief summary of financial results and achievements to date.

Suggested further reading

The Entrepreneur's Complete Self-Assessment Guide, Douglas A Gray, Kogan Page, 1987.

How to Form a Private Company, Alex Just, Jordans, 1985.

Starting a Workers' Cooperative, Mark Roberts, the Cooperative Development Agency.

Starting in Business, Form IR28, from the Board of Inland Revenue.

Allied Dunbar Tax Guide, annual, W I Sinclair, Longman, (covers in detail tax requirements of sole traders, partnerships and limited companies).

Choosing and Using Professional Advisers, revised edition, ed Paul Chaplin, Kogan Page, 1986.

The Stoy Hayward Business Tax Guide, annual, Mavis Seymour and Stephen Say, Kogan Page.

Assignment 3
A Description of Your
Products or Services

Here you should describe what products or services you propose to market, what stage of development they are at and why they are competitive with existing sources of supply. Part of the information in this section is for the benefit of outside readers who may not be familiar with your business. It should also be useful to you since the research and analysis required will encourage you to examine your offering *vis-à-vis* your competitors'.

Explore these topics in this section of your business plan:

Description of products and/or services

Explain what it is you are selling. Be specific and avoid unnecessary jargon. The reader should end up with more than just a vague idea about your products and/or services. Obviously, some products and services will require much more explanation than others. If you have invented a new process for analysing blood you will need to provide the reader with many details. On the other hand, if you are selling your services as a bookkeeper, you may need to do little more than list the services you will provide. A danger of this section is in assuming that the reader can easily understand your products without your providing sufficient detail and description.

PNU-CLEEN, a new industrial cleaner aimed specifically at the metal machining, wood-working and textile manufacturing industries, included in their business plan this description of the product:

'The method of producing the suction in the cleaner is very simple. The technical term is a 'jet-pump'. In reality this is just a stream of high velocity air passed into a tube. It is a very similar device to the vacuum pumps found on the taps in chemistry laboratories but a 'jet-pump' uses air as the prime mover instead of water (compressed air is readily available in most manufacturing units). The high speed air, when passing down the tube, will accelerate the surrounding air in the tube and draw air into the tube, similar to the draw of a chimney, causing a 'vacuum' effect, an area of lower than atmospheric pressure.

The air is accelerated by a small annular inlet supplied by a manifold surrounding the inlet. The air is controlled by a simple on/off valve. Incorporated into the valve is another position which allows for the provision of a supply of high speed air to be used to clean out difficult to get at areas and to dislodge swarf from awkward places.

Once the dirt/swarf/chippings have been picked up by the vacuum and past the position of the inlet of accelerated air the dirt/swarf/chippings are blown down a flexible pipe. This blowing action is much stronger than the vacuum and means that the flexible pipe will never get blocked. It also means that the pipe can be of considerable length. In practice the length will be limited to between 2 and 3 metres to stop it getting in the way and allow for easy handling.

The tube is clipped over the side of an existing dustbin where the air and dirt/swarf/chippings are separated out using a simple filter in order to stop the dirt/swarf/chippings being blown straight out of the dustbin again.'

In addition to listing and describing your products and/or services, you should note any applications or uses of your products that are not readily apparent to the reader. For instance, a photocopier can also produce overhead transparencies, as well as its more mundane output. When you make your list, show the proportion of turnover you expect each product or service to contribute to the whole, as illustrated below.

Product/service	Description	% of sales
		100%

Readiness for market

Are your products and/or services available for sale now? If not, what needs to be done to develop them? If you are selling a product, does it require more design work or research and development? Have you actually produced one or more completed products?

When Mark Saunders, a 1985 Cranfield enterprise programme participant put his proposal for the Strida, a revolutionary folding bicycle, before

45

the venture capital panel, the only projections he could include with any degree of certainty were costs.

The business proposal for which he sought backing was to take his brainchild from the drawing board, to a properly costed production prototype. For this he needed time, about two years, living expenses for that period, the use of a workshop and a modest amount of materials.

Saunders's business plan detailed how he would develop the product over this period and as a result the concept was backed by James Marshall, one-time manager of golfer Greg Norman. Marshall put together the manufacturing and marketing elements of the business plan, and by Christmas 1987 the Strida was in full-scale production and on sale through stores such as Harrods, Next Essentials, John Lewis, House of Fraser, Kelvin Hughes and many others.

If you are selling a service, do you presently have the skills and technical capability to provide it? If not, what needs to be done?

If additional inputs are required before your products or services are ready to be sold, state both the tasks to be done and time required, as shown below.

Product/service	State of development	Tasks to be done	Completion date

Proprietary position

Do your products or services have any special competitive advantage? If so, explain the advantages and state how long this proprietary position is likely to last. You should state any other factors that give you a competitive advantage, even though the advantage is not protected by contractual agreements of the law. Examples could include a special skill or talent not easily obtainable by others. (If you have none of these, and many businesses do not, do not just make something up!)

When Peter King (38) and Len Maxwell (28) had a good idea, they spent several months perfecting it and found themselves with a completely unique product. What was the next step?

'We had found a niche in the market and realised our product would satisfy it.' However, the ensuing product 'Videoalert', a simple but ingenious video security system, was easy to copy. The size of two video cassettes, it is attached to the side of the video recorder. Once the recorder is lifted or moved even a fraction, the alarm lets off an earpiercing shriek which will continue for eight hours.

The only way they could protect themselves from would-be imitators was to take out patents. As a further precaution they took out insurance against patent transgression, providing £250,000 for legal action. The patent for Videoalert was filed at the end of 1982 and in 1984 it was extended to the whole of Europe, South Africa, the USA, Canada, Australia and Israel. The Alert products factory in Coventry employs 18 people, turning out 250,000 Videoalerts each year.

If, like King and Maxwell, you have a unique business idea, you should investigate the four categories of protection: *patenting*, which protects technological and other inventions; *design registration*, which protects the shape or appearance of a commercial product; *copyright*, which protects literary, artistic and musical works; and *trade mark registration*, which protects symbols, logos and pictures.

Some products may be covered by two or more categories, eg the mechanism of a clock may be patented while its appearance may be design-registered.

Each category requires a different set of procedures, offers a different level of protection and extends for a different period of time. They all have one thing in common, though: in the event of any infringement your only redress is through the courts, and going to law can be wasteful of time and money, whether you win or lose.

Patents

A patent can be regarded as a contract between an inventor and the state. The state agrees with the inventor that if he is prepared to publish details of his invention in a set form and if it appears that he has made a real advance, the state will then grant him a 'monopoly' on his invention for 20 years: 'protection in return for disclosure'. The inventor uses the monopoly period to manufacture and sell his innovation; competitors can read the published specifications and glean ideas for their research, or they can approach the inventor and offer to help to develop his idea under licence.

However, the granting of a patent doesn't mean the proprietor is *automatically* free to make, use or sell the invention himself, since to do so might involve infringing an earlier patent which has not yet expired.

A patent really only allows the inventor to stop another person using the particular device which forms the subject of his patent. The state does not guarantee validity of a patent either, so it is not uncommon for patents to be challenged through the courts.

Which inventions can you patent? The basic rules are that an invention must be *new*, must involve an *inventive step* and must be capable of *industrial exploitation*.

You can't patent scientific/mathematical theories or mental processes, computer programs or ideas which might encourage offensive, immoral or anti-social behaviour. New medicines are patentable but not medical methods of treatment. Neither can you have just rediscovered a long forgotten idea (knowingly or unknowingly).

If you want to apply for a patent, it is essential not to disclose your idea in non-confidential circumstances. If you do, your invention is already 'published' in the eyes of the law, and this could well invalidate your application.

There are two distinct stages in the patenting process:

- from filing an application up to publication of the patent
- from publication to grant of the patent.

Two fees are payable for the first part of the process and a further fee for the second part. The whole process takes some two and a half years. Relevant forms and details of how to patent are available free of charge from the Patent Office.

It is possible – and cheaper – to make your own patent application but this is not really recommended. Drafting a specification to give you as wide a monopoly as you think you can get away with is the essence of patenting and this is the skill of professional patent agents. They also know the tricks of the trade for each stage of the patenting procedure. A list of patent agents is available from the Chartered Institute of Patent Agents.

What can you do with your idea? If you have dreamt up an inspired invention but don't have the resources, skill, time or inclination to produce it yourself, you can take one of three courses once the idea is patented:

1. *Outright sale.* You can sell the rights and title of your patent to an individual or company. The payment you ask should be based on a sound evaluation of the market.
2. *Sale and royalty.* You can enter into an agreement whereby you assign

the title and rights to produce the product to another party for cash but under which you get a royalty on each unit sold.

> Anthony Robinson, the inventor of Holomedia, a novel hologram display system, decided while on a Cranfield enterprise programme not to make and market his product himself. Instead, he sold the patented product to a large established company in a complementary field for a substantial six figure sum, a £20,000 pa retainer and continuing royalties. His business now is concentrated exclusively on developing innovative products for other companies to make and sell.

3. *Licensing.* You keep the rights and title but sell a licence for manufacturing and marketing the product to someone else. The contract between you and the licensee should contain a performance clause requiring the licensee to sell a minimum number of units each year or the licence will be revoked.

Whichever option you select, you need a good patent agent/lawyer on your side.

Trade marks

A trade mark is the symbol by which the goods of a particular manufacturer or trader can be identified. Trade marks can be a word, a signature, a monogram, a picture, a logo or a combination of these.

To qualify for registration the trade mark must be distinctive, must not be deceptive and must not be capable of confusion with marks already registered. Excluded are misleading marks, national flags, royal crests, insignia of the armed forces. A trade mark can only apply to tangible goods, not services (although pressure is mounting for this to be changed).

The Trade Marks Act of 1938 offers protection of great commercial value since, unlike other forms of protection, your sole rights to use the trade mark continue indefinitely.

To register a trade mark you or your agent should first conduct preliminary searches at the Trade Marks Branch of the Patent Office to check there are no conflicting marks already in existence. You then apply for registration on the official trade mark form and pay a fee (currently £42).

Your application is then advertised in the weekly *Trade Marks Journal* to allow any objections to be raised. If there are none, your trade mark will be officially registered and you pay a further fee (currently £53).

Registration is initially for seven years. After this, it can be renewed for periods of 14 years at a time, with no upper time limit.

It isn't mandatory to register a trade mark. If an unregistered trade mark has been used for some time and could be construed as closely associated with the product by customers, it will have acquired a 'reputation' which will give it some protection legally, but registration makes it much simpler for the owner to have recourse against any person who infringes the mark.

Design registration

You can register the shape, design or decorative features of a commercial product if it is new, original, never published before or – if already known – never before applied to the product you have in mind. Protection is intended to apply to industrial articles to be produced in quantities of more than 50. Design registration only applies to features which appeal to the eye – not to the way the article functions.

To register a design, you should apply to the Design Registry and send a specimen or photograph of the design plus a registration fee (currently £44). This is examined to see whether it is new or original and complies with other requirements of the Registered Designs Act 1949. If it does, a certification of registration is issued which gives you, the proprietor, the sole right to manufacture, sell or use in business articles of that design.

Protection lasts for five years but can be renewed for two further five-year periods. You can handle the design registration yourself but, again, it might be preferable to let a specialist do it for you. There is no register of design agents but most patent agents are well versed in design law.

> Paul Smith, the designer, started up his men's fashion business in Covent Garden in 1977, and within a decade he had developed it into a worldwide venture worth a conservative £13 million. The clothes sold in high street chains, and men's sections in department stores in Britain and abroad slavishly imitate the Paul Smith label. Pirates find his designs irresistible: only recently Smith won £5000 damages against the menswear company Reiss for their blatant copy of one of his sweaters. He sued, he says, 'just to let them know I knew'. Normally he simply turns a blind eye, wryly amused that, 'without realising it, I've started huge business for other people'.

Copyright

Copyright is a complex field and since it is unlikely to be relevant to most business start-ups we only touch on it lightly here.

Basically, the Copyright Act 1956 gives protection against the unlicensed copying of original artistic and creative works – articles, books, paintings, films, plays, songs, music, engineering drawings. To claim copyright the item in question should carry this symbol: © (author's name) (date).

You can take the further step of recording the date on which the work was completed (plus a £23 fee) with the Registrar at Stationers Hall. This, though, is an unusual precaution to take and probably only necessary if you anticipate an infringement.

Copyright protection in the UK lasts for 50 years after the death of the person holds the copyright, or 50 years after publication if this is later.

Copyright is infringed only if more than a 'substantial' part of your work is reproduced (ie issued for sale to the public) without your permission, but since there is no formal registration of copyright the question of whether or not your work is protected usually has to be decided in a court of law.

Sources of further information

Patent Office, State House, 66–71 High Holborn, London WC1R 4TP; 01-831 2525 (open to public Mon-Fri 10am-4pm). Publishes the following pamphlets: *Applying for a patent, Introducing patents – a guide for inventors, How to prepare a UK patent application.*

Design Registry, 11th Floor, State House, 66–71 High Holborn, London WC1R 4TP; 01-831 2525. Publishes free of charge guides to registering designs.

Trade Marks Registry, State House, 66–71 High Holborn, London WC1R 4TP (Mon-Fri 10am-4pm). Publishes free of charge: *Applying for a trade mark; Trade Marks Journal* (every Wednesday).

Stationers Hall, Ave Maria Lane, Ludgate Hill, London EC4M 7DD; 01-248 2934 (Mon-Fri 10am-4pm) for registration of copyright. Provides details and forms for registration.

The Chartered Institute of Patent Agents, Staple Inn Buildings, High Holborn, London WC1V 7PX; 01-405 9450. No advisory service but will put you in contact with a patent agent in your area. Publishes a Register of Patent Agents which lists names and business addresses of all patent agents qualified to practise before the Patent Office.

Institute of Patentees & Inventors, Suite 505A, Triumph House, 189 Regent Street, London W1R 7WF; 01-242 7812. A membership organisation (membership costs £30 pa). Looks after the interests of patent holders and inventors. Can provide useful advice and guidance on almost every aspect of intellectual property from idea conception to innovation and development. Publishes quarterly journal and *New Patents Bulletin*. The latter acts as liaison with industry, bringing members' inventions to the notice of specialised manufacturing firms.

Institute of Trade Mark Agents, Suite 3, Panther House, 38 Mount Pleasant, London WC1X 0AP; 01-833 0875. Can put you in contact with a trade mark agent in your area and give general advice. Shortly to produce a register of trade marks.

Comparison with competitive products and services

Identify those products and/or services that you think will be competing with yours. They may be similar products/services or they may be quite different, but could be substituted for yours. An example of the latter would be a business which sells copying machines, which competes not only against other copying machines, but also against carbon paper and copy shops.

Once you have identified the major competing products, compare yours against them. List the advantages and disadvantages of yours *vis-à-vis* the competition. Later on, when you do your market research, you will probably want to address this question again and revise this section.

After making the comparison draw your conclusions. If your products/services will compete effectively, explain why. If not, explain what you plan to do to make them compete.

Returning to PNU CLEEN Ltd, their business plan presented to the Cranfield enterprise panel included the following statement explaining their competitive advantage:

'As such there is no direct competition for the cleaner. This must be qualified by saying that there are some designs of vacuum cleaner that offer some but not all of the benefits that this design offers. The closest is a product made by Alpha Components Limited but it is based on a very small bore, almost unworkable.

There is considerable indirect competition from electrically powered vacuum cleaners, pneumatic vacuum cleaners and the dustpan and brush. Overcoming this indirect competition should be achieved by making the customer aware that this cleaner is designed especially for use alongside a machine or workstation and offers the most convenient method at a low cost of keeping a high standard of cleanliness.'

Guarantees and warranties

Will you be providing either of these with your product or service? Describe both the scope of the warranty or guarantee, what it may cost, the benefits you expect from providing it, and how it will work in practice.

Possible future developments

If your product or service lends itself to other opportunities, with relatively minor alteration, which can be achieved quickly and will enhance your business, briefly describe these ideas.

Some product turn-offs

Is one product enough?

One-product businesses are the natural output of the inventor, but they are extremely vulnerable to competition, changes in fashion and to technological obsolescence. Having only one product can also limit the growth potential of the enterprise. A question mark must inevitably hang over such ventures until they can broaden out their product base.

Single-sale products

Medsoft was a business founded to sell a micro-computer and a tailor-made software package to hospital doctors. Unfortunately, the management had no idea of the cost and effort required to sell each unit. Worse still, there were no repeat sales. It was not that customers did not like the product: they did, but each user needed only one product. This meant that all the money and time spent on building up a 'loyal' customer was largely wasted.

In another type of venture, for example selling company cars, you could reasonably expect a satisfied customer to come back every two or three years. In the restaurant business the repeat purchase cycle might be every two to three months.

Non-essential products

Entrepreneurs tend to be attracted to fad, fashion and luxury items because of the short response time associated with their promotion and sale. Companies producing for these markets frequently run into financial difficulties arising out of sudden market shifts. Market security is more readily gained by having products that are viewed as 'essential'.

Worlds of Wonder was founded only in 1985, and immediately boomed. Sales in its second full year increased by 252 per cent to $327 million, and profits by 130 per cent, on the back of two blockbuster products – Teddy

Ruxpin, a talking bear, and Lazer Tag, a game of catch using laser beams and sensors.

Worlds of Wonder's mistake was in failing to shield itself against the fickleness of blockbusters. Its choice for 1987 was Julie, a hi-tech doll which responded to a child's voice, a genus known in the trade as 'interactive plush'. Technically imperfect and costing a high $100, Julie was an interactive flop with parents whose pockets proved less malleable than children's desires. WOW had nothing else to fall back on, and so – like other and earlier toy makers – it just fell.

The toy business is now wickedly competitive. There is no shortage of entrepreneurs developing the greatest game since Scrabble and the best doll since Barbie. Margins are thin and entry costs low.

Diversification can be the best course for a firm with a blockbuster, rather than betting that its designers will have another winner next year. Coleco put $60 million of its earnings from Cabbage Patch Dolls (the hit of 1985) into buying the American makers of Trivial Pursuit, Scrabble and Talking Wrinkles, an electronic puppy. That has revived Coleco's sales, but not yet reversed losses from 1986. More diversified still, Fisher-Price, a wizard with pre-school toys, is owned by Quaker Oats. In such a group the toy maker becomes a high-risk fling with part of group profits. If children turn away, the company can survive.

Too simple a product

Simplicity, usually a desirable feature, can be a drawback. If a business idea is so basic that little management or marketing expertise is required for success, this is likely to make the cost of entry low and the value added minimal. This makes it easy for every Tom, Dick or Harry to duplicate the product idea, and impossible for the original company to defend its market, except by lowering the price.

The video rental business was a classic example of the 'too simple product' phenomenon. Too many people jumped on the bandwagon as virtually anyone with a couple of thousand pounds could set themselves up. Rental prices fell from pounds to pence in a year or so, and hundreds of businesses folded.

The founder of Charter (Self-Assembly Furniture) Ltd included this product description in his business plan:

> The system at present allows the construction of chairs, tables, cup-boards, chests of drawers, wardrobes, beds, a cot, climbing frame etc, in fact conceivably any item of furniture that a strong box-frame structure can be, or is required to be, an essential part of.
>
> The crux of the system is an easily screwed together (by hand, no tools required) jointing method, that imparts rigidity and strength while being only hand tight. An aim of the design was to keep as many components as possible common to each item of furniture, so that certain items could evolve by additional follow-up purchases. An example of this idea would be the progression from cot through to playpen, then to climbing frame,

some components of the latter being usable in other items such as shelves or chairs. Another aim was to enable the transformation from one item to another to be very simply and very rapidly achieved.

The system will be available in a variety of solid woods or, where appropriate, veneered or laminated synthetic boards like medium density fibreboard (MDF). Metal fittings, where required, eg hinges, clips and holders, will be sturdy but discreet and, where possible, not visible externally.

The appearance is modern, though not avant-garde, with a style expected to be favoured by the groups identified as being the most likely purchasers. The natural style, as a consequence of the method of construction, would not be out of place in a Habitat store.

To summarise, the major features of this system which help to distinguish it are:

1. Speed of assembly.
2. Simplicity of assembly: no tools are required in the assembly of any piece – tools are only required for wall mounting of shelves or units and in these instances the design minimises the number of drilled holes required and maximises the simplicity of hanging.
3. Attractive 'up-market' appearance of the assembled item.
4. Consumer choice in the overall dimensions of the piece where possible, eg height of chairs, size and design of climbing frames, size and spacing of shelves in shelf system and room dividers.
5. Sturdiness – something missing from much self-assembly furniture (SAF).
6. The buy as you go along feature, especially of the shelf systems and climbing frames.
7. Ease and standardisation of manufacture. This should minimise manufacturing costs and offer the option of passing on the consequential benefit to the consumer.

I am at present investigating the possibility of patenting certain aspects of the way in which the elements of this furniture system are put together. A preliminary search at the Patent Office produced an optimistic result and a subsequent discussion with a Patent Agent confirmed that this is a real possibility. To get satisfactory protection for the product in the major European markets will cost around £20,000.

Worksheet for Assignment 3: A description of your products or services

1. Describe your product or service, as if explaining it to a novice.
2. Is it currently available for sale? If not, what needs to be done, how much will that work cost and how long will it take?
3. Do you have, or plan to have, any legal protection such as patents? If so, explain what you have done so far to establish your rights.
4. How is your product or service different from those already on the market?

5. Will you be providing any warranties, guarantees or after-sales service?
6. Are there any possibilities of developing new products or services complementary to the one(s) described above?

Suggested further reading

A Manager's Guide to Patents, Trade Marks and Copyright, John F Williams, Kogan Page, 1986.

Phase 2
Market Research

Introduction

Assignments 4-6 are intended to help you to bring your customers, competitors and the market-place more sharply into focus, and to identify areas you have yet to research.

The Duke of Wellington defined reconnaissance as the 'art of knowing what is on the other side of the hill'. Market research is the business equivalent of this military activity. It is the name given to the process of collecting, recording, classifying and analysing data on customers, competitors and any other influences in the chain that links buyers to sellers.

The research should be done *before* the business is started or a new strategy is pursued, so saving the time and cost incurred if expensive mistakes are made. Obviously, the amount of research undertaken has to be related to the sums at risk. If a venture calls for a start-up investment of £1000, spending £5000 on market research would be a bad investment. However, new and small businesses that do not want to join the catastrophically high first-year failure statistics would be prudent to carry out some elementary market research, whatever level their start-up capital is to be.

As the President of the Harvard Business School said: 'If you think knowledge is expensive, try ignorance.'

The data collected in this phase can be used to help you to decide on an appropriate strategy for your business.

The starting point in any market research has to be a definition of the scope of the market you are aiming for. A small general shop may only service the needs of a few dozen streets. A specialist restaurant may have to call on a much larger catchment area to be viable.

You may eventually decide to sell to different markets. For example, a retail business can serve a local area through the shop and a national area by mail order. A small manufacturing business could branch out into exporting.

People all too often flounder in their initial market research by describing their markets too broadly. For example, saying that they are in the motor industry when they really mean they sell second-hand cars in Perth; or in health foods, when they are selling wholemeal bread from a village shop.

While it is important to be aware of trends in the wider market this must not obscure the need to focus on the precise area that you have to serve.

Shirt Point

Started just before Christmas 1987, it is the brainchild of adman Robert Barclay and his friend since primary school, art dealer Jeremy Wayne. 'We were having lunch 18 months ago and complaining about the hassle we had trying to get shirts done,' says Barclay, aged 29. 'High performers in the City, earning perhaps £100,000 a year and working from 7am until 7pm, still have to get up at the crack of dawn to iron a shirt.'

Their catchment area is initially being restricted to the City and they are already laundering up to 300 shirts a week, charging £1.65 apiece. It means hard-pressed brokers and bankers can take their dirty laundry to the office, telephone Shirt Point, have it collected the same day and returned, hand-finished with buttons sewn on and collar bones renewed where necessary, within 48 hours.

Assignments 4 and 5 pose the main questions you need to answer concerning your customers and competitors, and Assignment 6 covers the principal ways in which basic market research can be conducted, and where such data can be found.

Assignment 4
Customers

Without customers no business can get off the ground, let alone survive. Some people believe that customers arrive after the firm 'opens its doors'. This is nonsense. You need a clear idea of who your customers will be in advance, as they are a vital component of a successful business strategy, not simply the passive recipients of new products or services.

Knowing something about your customers and what you plan to sell to them seems so elementary it is hard to believe that any potential business person could start a business without doing so. But it is all too common – and one of the reasons why many new businesses fail.

Here's a story which illustrates the pitfalls:

In 1982 Tim Johnston took voluntary redundancy and decided to start his own business. His redundancy money combined with his savings gave him a total of £15,000, which he put into a vending machine business. He chose vending since he thought that with the demise of the tea lady it must be a growth market.

He surveyed the vending machine manufacturers and selected three machines that were easy to maintain and simple to fill and clean. He bought demonstration models at a discount, and installed them in his newly acquired office-cum-storeroom. He then looked for suppliers of ingredients, paying particular attention to the flavours since he believed that vended drinks had a poor reputation.

Next he arranged with two leasing companies a deal by which they would finance the machines he sold to satisfactory customers.

All this took Tim four months and, by the autumn of 1982, he felt certain that he had a good product to offer.

He then started to sell. First he called on established medium-sized local companies. It quickly became clear that they already either had a vending machine or well-rehearsed reasons for not wanting one. So Tim moved downmarket and went to see small and new companies – and immediately hit a new problem. The leasing companies he had lined up would only take on clients with a good financial track record. Otherwise they required the directors of the company to provide personal guarantees in case the company defaulted. Now Tim had not only to persuade customers to buy a vending machine but to abandon the shelter of limited liability to do so!

By the end of the first month of his sales campaign, Tim had called on 250 people, seen 28 and given two quotes for machines.

His next tack was to identify likely prospects via the telephone, but the closest he got to an order was from a firm that wanted a vending machine to provide refreshments for night-shift workers. The firm didn't care twopence about the quality of the ingredients; its only concern was that the machine could dispense all night on a single fill of drinks.

After six months 'in business' Tim closed down. Nearly half his cash was gone and he hadn't got a single order.

What do customers need?

The founder of a successful cosmetics firm, when asked what his business did, replied, 'In the factories we make perfume and in the shops we sell dreams.'

Business people usually define their business in physical terms. Customers, on the other hand, see businesses as satisfying their needs. Compare a Bic with a Parker pen. Basically they are very similar: they both write well, are comfortable to hold, have clips that hold them in place and caps that protect your pockets from ink stains. One costs 10p, the other £3. Customers pay the extra £2.90 for largely intangible benefits such as status or the pleasure the pen will bring as a gift. Bic and Parker are both successful businesses, but the needs they satisfy are poles apart.

Until you have clearly defined the needs of your potential customers, you cannot begin to assemble a product to satisfy them.

In Hugh McNicholl's opinion, his customers expect style. The philosophy might appear strange for someone in the mountaineering equipment business, but the success of his company Mountain Technology (Glencoe) proves otherwise.

In the outdoor sports boom in the West, producing a technically adequate product is no longer enough, he says. With more and more people climbing mountains for fun rather than machismo, 'aesthetic' aspects are becoming just as important when it comes to winning the market over, says Mr McNicholl, whose main line is the manufacture of his own design of ice axe. 'Appearance is a big thing,' he adds. 'I've been able to combine functional quality with a really good looking, nononsense design. I'm selling – and taking business away from the big boys.'

The 'big boys' are the French, Austrians and Germans, who until now have cornered the world market. However, in the four years since his firm was founded in 1981, Mr McNicholl has lured away 20 per cent of the UK market in ice axes, estimated at up to 10,000 sales a year.

The American psychologist Maslow says that 'all customers are goal seekers who gratify their needs by purchase and consumption'. He classifies consumer needs in a five-stage pyramid, called the hierarchy of needs:

Self-realisation
Self-esteem
Social
Safety
Physiological (hunger and thirst)

Every product or service is bought to satisfy one or more of these needs. So, for example, as people's hunger and thirst needs are satisfied, they move up the hierarchy to satisfy other needs.

Try interesting someone who is starving and cold in 'higher' things; or see how much more food you buy if you shop when you are hungry than when you have just consumed a large meal.

Where are your customers on the needs hierarchy, and how can your product or service help them to achieve their goals?

Segmenting the market

Market segmentation is the name given to the process whereby customers and potential customers are organised into clusters or groups of 'similar' types. For example, a shop or restaurant has regulars and passing trade. The balance between the two is a fundamental issue that affects everything the business does.

Also, each of these customer groups is motivated to buy for different reasons and your selling message has to be modified accordingly.

These are some of the ways by which markets can be segmented:

Demographic segmentation groups customers together by such variables as age, sex, education and income. One owner of a corner shop identified two particular groups of customers: schoolchildren, and housewives who had run out of products they would normally buy from a supermarket. For the former the products on offer are sweets, comics, pencils and cheap games. For the latter, small sizes of such items as butter, cereal and washing powder.

Benefit segmentation recognises that different people get different satisfaction from the same product or service. Most toothpaste manufacturers stress the 'benefit' of decay protection, such as the claim, 'Look mum, no cavities.' However, others reach a quite different market with their 'whiteness' message. White teeth, with the implied attractiveness to the opposite sex, is a more important benefit to some customers.

Geographic segments arise when customer preferences vary by location. For example, the photocopy shop and the motorcycle despatch rider are very much 'products' of a city environment.

There are useful rules to help you decide on whether a market segment is worth trying to sell into.

- *Measurability.* Can you estimate how many customers are in the segment?
- *Accessibility.* Can you communicate with these customers? Just knowing 'they are out there somewhere' is not much help.
- *Size.* A segment has to have a 'large' number of customers, although exactly what constitutes large will be relative to your business.
- *Open to practical development.* Just being a large segment is not enough. The customer must have money to spend and be able to spend it. Some government departments, for example, are restricted to buying from 'approved' suppliers only. So they may be large, but of no interest at all if you cannot sell to them.

In other cases government regulations themselves are the problem, as one young entrepreneur found to his cost.

Britain's 28 million telephone users are being prevented from buying a unique electronic lock to keep their bills under control. The device, which can be programmed to allow some calls and stop others, cannot be put on the market because of red tape.

The lock is the creation of Terry Newell, a Leicester-based designer who says it could have been on sale in 1986. He invented it in 1982, has spent £100,000 on lawyers, patents and design fees, but is unable to offer it to the public because the authorities cannot decide what standards it should meet.

To be made in Britain it needs to have official approval. But he cannot obtain this unless it meets certain standards, and nobody can tell Newell what standards to meet because they have not been decided.

A body called the TCL2 committee, with members from throughout the telecommunications industry, has been debating the matter since 1985, but without success. A British standard for call-barring apparatus was due to be approved by the committee in February 1987 but this did not happen and little progress has been made.

Newell's invention, which would sell for less than £40, is wired into a telephone socket and activated by dialling a four-figure code. Intended for homes and small businesses, it can be programmed to exclude international and long-distance calls, for example, or all calls except 999.

Parents could use the device to prevent au pairs telephoning home, or children calling expensive services like Talkabout, British Telecom's chatline. A shop could set it to allow calls only to predetermined numbers, such as credit card companies, a taxi firm and head office.

In many countries, telephone users can choose from a range of call-barring devices, some of which are also on sale here. But they are not approved for connection to Britain's telephone network and users risk a £2000 fine.

Segmentation is an important marketing process, as it helps to bring customers more sharply into focus, and it classifies them into manageable groups. It has wide-ranging implications for other marketing decisions. For example, the same product can be priced differently according to the intensity of customers' needs. The first- and second-class post is one example, off-peak rail travel another.

It is also a continuous process that needs to be carried out periodically, for example when strategies are being reviewed.

Bridget Woods, famous for Strawberry Studio (the fashion label that she started at 19), now presides over a high profile empire with a £5 million annual turnover. 'My talent is for seeing gaps in the market, and believing that my ideas will work.'

Her first taste of success was during college days when she teamed up with fellow fashion student, George Hammer. 'We started to sell designer jeans through mail order ads in *Melody Maker*. It took off, so we converted my parents' loft into a dispatch room and began to wholesale to shops in the King's Road.' After qualifying, they borrowed £1700 from the bank, and in 1973 launched Strawberry Studio with a collection featuring bright fifties skirts and boned tops. Department stores, bored by years of denim, jumped to attention, and orders poured in.

By 1980 Strawberry Studio was a household name, but then came the recession and sales dropped. Bridget reacted by launching a new upmarket label aimed at people whose pockets had more of an inflation-proof lining. The collection was snapped up and the company was saved.

Defining the product in the customers' terms

Once you know what you are selling and to whom, you can match the features of the product (or service) to the benefits that customers will get when they purchase. *Features* are what a product has or is, and *benefits* are what the product does for the customer. Finally, as in the example overleaf, include 'proof' that these benefits can be delivered.

Features	Benefits	Proofs
We use a unique hardening process for our machine	Our tools last longer and that saves you money	- We have a patent on the process
which means that	*you can see this is true because*	- Independent tests carried out by the Cambridge Institute of Technology show our product lasts longest
Our shops stay open later than others in the area	You get more choice when to shop	Come and see
Our computer system is fault tolerant using parallel processing	You have no downtime for either defects or system expansion	- Our written specification guarantees this - Come and talk to satisfied customers operating in your field

Remember, the customer pays for the benefits and the seller for the features.

Who will buy first?

Customers do not sit and wait for a new business to open its doors. Word spreads slowly as the message is diffused throughout the various customer groups. Even then it is noticeable that generally it is the more adventurous types that first buy from a new business. Only after these people have given their seal of approval do the 'followers' come along.

This adoption process, from the 2.5 per cent of innovators who make up a new business's first customers, through to the laggards who won't buy from anyone until they have been in business for 20 years, is most noticeable with innovative products, such as micro-computers, but the general trend is true for all businesses.

Until you have sold to the innovators significant sales cannot be achieved. So an important first task is to identify these customers. The moral is: the more you know about your potential customers at the outset, the better your chances of success.

At the minimum, your business plan should include information on:

1. Who your principal customers are or, if you are launching into new areas, who they are likely to be. Determine in as much detail as you think appropriate the income, age, sex, education, interests, occupation and marital status of your potential customers, and name names if at all possible.

> Anthony Wreford, now aged 35, started his PR company in 1981. He and partner Michael McAvoy invested £5000 each, hired a secretary and rented three rooms in Mayfair. For the next two years they spent every waking moment getting McAvoy Wreford off the ground. 'We went through our complete list of contacts and invited anyone relevant over for lunch. To avoid wasting time, it became a standing joke to only deal with a MAN, which is shorthand for clients who have the Money, Authority and Need.'
>
> After four years they were approached with a brilliant buy-out offer. Two years and a performance-related contract later, Wreford and McAvoy knew that they were millionaires.

2. What factors are important in the customer's decision to buy or not to buy *your* product and/or service, how much they should buy and how frequently?

> Together with her husband, Richard Ross, Sophie Mirman is founder of Sock Shops, a hosiery chain started in Knightsbridge Underground station in 1983 and floated on the Unlisted Securities Market in May this year for more than £27 million. Today she has more than 50 outlets. Aged 30 and with one daughter, she started her career as a secretary at Marks and Spencer, then moved to the specialist retailers Tie Rack where she met her husband. Mirman attributes her success to the simple fact that, 'we supply a necessity at convenient locations and at equally convenient trading hours'.
>
> Tom Farmer, the son of a Leith shipping clerk who earned £5 a week, launched Kwik-Fit in 1971. By 1986 the company had a turnover of £125 million, made £15 million profit, and employed 2400 people by servicing three and a half million cars a year. In his own words, the enduring philosophy behind his business, to which he ascribes its success, is, '100 per cent customer satisfaction. Just giving service – phoning back in half-an-hour if you say you will, standing by promises – puts you miles ahead of anyone else in the field.'

Many factors probably have an influence and it is often not easy to identify all of them. These are some of the common ones that you should consider investigating:

(a) *Product considerations*

- Price
- Quality
- Appearance (colour, texture, shape, materials etc)
- Packaging
- Size
- Fragility, ease of handling, transportability
- Servicing, warranty, durability
- Operating characteristics (efficiency, economy, adaptability etc)

(b) *Business considerations*

- Location and facilities
- Reputation
- Method(s) of selling
- Opening hours, delivery times etc
- Credit terms
- Advertising and promotion
- Variety of goods and/or services on offer
- Appearance and/or attitude of company's property and/or employees
- Capability of employees

(c) *Other considerations*

- Weather, seasonality, cyclicality
- Changes in the economy – recession, depression, boom

Since many of these factors relate to the attitudes and opinions of the potential customers, it is likely that answers to these questions will only be found through interviews with customers. It is also important to note that many factors that affect buying are not easily researched and are even less easy to act upon. For example, the amount of light in a shop or the position of a product on the shelves can influence buying decisions.

You could perhaps best use the above list to rate what potential customers see as your strengths and weaknesses. Then see if you can use that information to make your offering more appealing to them.

3. As well as knowing something of the characteristics of the likely buyers of your product or service, you also need to know how many of them there are, and whether their ranks are swelling or contracting. Overall market size, history and forecasts are important market research data that you need to assemble – particularly data

that refers to your chosen market segments, rather than just to the market as a whole.

Character (Self-Assembly Furniture) Ltd

Philip Waddell researched published data on the self-assembly furniture market and conducted his own research via a questionnaire. Some of his conclusions as to the profile of customers for his products were:

1. Nearly 26 per cent of all men had assembled furniture from flat packs in the past 12 months – 53 per cent had done so at some time.
2. 30 per cent of men had put up fitted shelves and cupboards in the past year – 60 per cent at some time in the recent past.
3. Over 75 per cent of these DIYers were in the 25-44 year age group.
4. Social groups A, B, C1 and C2 featured prominently, with the ABs significantly less interested than the Cs.
5. Owner-occupiers, especially those who had recently moved house, were most active in DIY, and in general people living in modern family housing on incomes 30 per cent or more higher than the national average.
6. 79 per cent said they would prefer DIY if the task was within their capabilities, in order to save money.
7. Women, in particular those who are married in the AB social class, aged between 25 and 34 are generally favourably disposed to the concept of DIY.
8. There is a strong correlation between involvement in home decorating and a willingness to buy self-assembly furniture. This has important connotations for advertising and distribution.
9. The main reasons cited for not buying self-assembly furniture are: lack of knowledge, lack of confidence and lack of time. This suggests that if the DIY task could be made evidently simpler and less time-consuming, then the numbers of people prepared to buy could be greatly increased.

The Oriental martial arts and fitness centre

The Oriental, a martial arts and fitness centre situated in the city of Cambridge, aims to provide specialised facilities for martial arts clubs, not at present available in Cambridge.

According to the recently published 'Sport in Cambridge', sports and leisure generates £4.4 billion of consumer spending per annum and 376,000 jobs. Recent growth in indoor sports has been linked with the growth in facilities, currently in the order of 1500 public sports centres and halls in the UK.

The Martial Arts Commission membership figures show a growth in membership from 28,000 members in 1979 to 106,000 in 1986. These figures do not include members of the British Judo Association, which had 41,700 members in 1986, an increase of 1365 over the previous year, or most self-defence classes which have no governing body. 77 per cent of martial arts instructors questionnaired reported increasing interest in their martial art; none reported decreasing interest.

The growth of fitness and exercise participation alongside sports in the last 20 years with the popularity of jogging, fun running, weight training and aerobics has been the fastest growing area for women's activities. A Sports Council survey suggests that 2.4 million women take part regularly in movement and dance and that 10 per cent of women take part in aerobics and keep fit.

Customer benefits

The benefits offered by the centre will be those of a well equipped training area, large enough comfortably to hold courses and competitions for at least 200 people. The centre will specialise in martial arts, but will also be suitable for dance and keep fit.

For the primary customer, ie martial arts clubs, the centre offers the highest quality training facilities for their needs in the area at affordable rates, and will promote their martial art, thus increasing participation levels.

For the secondary customer, ie the student of martial arts and participants in the other classes, the centre offers training in a pleasant atmosphere with good changing and showering facilities, a bar for relaxing in after training and a handy shop where equipment and books may be purchased.

Selected market segments

Two areas of the leisure market have been selected for this venture. First, the martial arts sector and, second, the fitness (especially women's) sector.

The martial arts sector (including self-defence) covers the spectrum of income/occupation groups, drawing from all walks of life. Judo has the highest proportion of junior participants (three-quarters of the members of the BJA), whereas the other martial arts show participants mainly in the 25–35 age range.

Students mainly practice twice weekly (50 per cent) with 30 per cent training three or four times weekly and a further 16 per cent training in excess of four times per week. 47 per cent of students attend courses at least twice in a year, most travelling to those close to home, with a few (27 per cent) prepared to travel further than 300 miles, including going overseas.

The keep-fit market is fairly well served in the evenings in Cambridge by the community colleges and sports hall. There is a gap in the women's weight training and in daytime classes for the unemployed or for mothers of younger children. This could be filled by offering crèche facilities during daytime classes.

Worksheet for Assignment 4: Customers

1. What is the geographic scope of the market you intend to serve and why have you so chosen?
2. What customer needs will your product or service satisfy?
3. List and describe the main different types of customer for your product/service.
4. Which of these market segments will you concentrate on and why?
5. Match the features of your product/service to the benefits on offer to customers in each of your chosen market segments. Provide proof, where possible.
6. Who are the innovators in each of your market segments?
7. What factors are important in the customer's decision to buy or not to buy your product/service?
8. Is the market you are aiming at currently rising or falling? What is the trend over the past few years?
9. What share of this market are you aiming for, initially?

Suggested further reading
Do Your Own Market Research, Paul Hague and Peter Jackson, Kogan Page, 1987.

Assignment 5
Competitors

Researching the competition is often a time-consuming and frustrating job, but there are important lessons to be learnt from it. Some of the information that would be of most value to you will not be available. Particularly hard to find is information relating to the size and profitability of your competitors. Businesses, and particularly smaller businesses, are very secretive about their finances. Because of this, you may have to make estimates of the size and profitability of various firms.

Research of competitors

When you begin your research, it is crucial that you make an accurate determination of your competitors. Remember, just because someone sells a similar product or service, that does not necessarily make him a competitor. Perhaps he makes the same product but sells it in an entirely different market. (By different market, we mean that it could be sold in a different geographical market, or to a different demographic market etc.) Just because someone sells a product or service that is different from yours does not mean that he is *not* a competitor. Completely dissimilar products are often substitutable for each other.

Once you have identified your competitors, you need to classify them further as to 'primary', 'secondary', 'potential' etc. There are two reasons for doing this. First, you need to limit the number of firms that you will do your research on to a workable number. If you try to research 25 firms in depth, you won't have time to do anything else. If you end up with more than 10 or 12 primary competitors, you should probably do your research on only a sample. Second, you may want to classify competitors into primary and secondary because your marketing strategy may be different for each group.

As mentioned previously, finding out the size and profitability of your competitors may be difficult. You may be able to get some valuable information from the annual accounts which each company has to file. However, you should be aware that these are often not filed when required, or they may be incomplete, or contain information of no value.

A second source of information is local business directories, eg Key British Enterprises, Kelly's etc. In addition to other types of information, these books list the category in which a particular company's sales volume falls. For instance, while it will not tell you the company's exact sales volume, it may tell you whether the company does less than £500,000–£1,000,000 etc.

Another way to find out size and profitability totals is to read the publications that cover the business scene. The financial section of your newspaper and trade magazines often contains stories that can be used for research.

If you have been unable to get the necessary information from published sources, try doing some primary research. Contact the company directly and ask them your questions. Usually, you will not get the information that you want but occasionally this approach does work. Next, contact the firm's suppliers, or other individuals who are in a position to know or estimate the information. Sometimes you can get a ballpark figure, if not an exact one, from a wholesaler or other supplier.

Finally, you may be able to make a reasonable estimate from the bits and pieces of information that you were able to collect. This is commonly done with the use of operating ratios. To illustrate, let us assume that you are researching a large restaurant. You are unable to find out its annual sales volume but after striking up a conversation with one of the employees you find out that the restaurant employs 40 full-time people. Because of your knowledge of the restaurant industry, you feel confident in estimating the restaurant's payroll at £240,000 a year. From a book that lists operating ratios for the restaurant industry, (published by the trade association) you find that payroll expenses, as a percentage of sales, average 40 per cent. With these facts you are able to estimate the annual sales volume of the restaurant at £600,000.

Several points should be noted here. First, operating ratios are published by a variety of trade associations and businesses. For most types of business they are not that difficult to obtain. Second, this approach is not limited to employment ratios. You can make estimates based upon inventory levels, rent, or other expenses. Third, learning to use this technique is not difficult. Once you understand the use and logic of ratio analysis, you should be able to make estimates like the above. These estimates are derived by doing ratio analysis in reverse. Instead of taking figures and working out the ratio, you start with the ratio and work out the figures. Fourth, the use of estimates resulting from this technique should be only a last resort, or used in conjunction with estimates derived in some other way. The reason for this is not that the ratio you found in the books may be 'average' but that the particular business may, for a variety of reasons, be far from average.

(See Assignment 13, Summary of performance ratios (page 189) for a description of the key operating and financial ratios.)

Useful addresses

Company Registration Office. Keeps financial records of all limited companies. For England and Wales these records are kept at Companies House, 55-71 City Road, London EC1Y 1BB; 01-253 9393. For Scotland at the Registrar of Companies, 102 George Street, Edinburgh EH2 3JD; 031-226 5774. For Northern Ireland at the Department of Commerce, Chichester House, 43-47 Chichester Court, Belfast BT1 4RJ; 0232 234121.

There are a number of commercial organisations who will obtain information from Companies House on your behalf for a modest fee. Two such organisations are:

The Company Search Centre
1-3 Leonard Street, London EC2A 4AQ
01-251 2566

Extel
37-45 Paul Street, London EC2A 4PB
01-253 3400

ICC Business Ratios 28-42 Banner Street, London EC1Y 8QU; 01-253 3906, produce 150 business sector reports analysing the performance of companies by providing 19 key business ratios, covering profitability, liquidity, gearing, asset utilisation, productivity, and growth rates.

Willings Press Guide published by Thomas Skinner Directors, Windsor Court, East Grinstead House, East Grinstead, West Sussex RH19 1XE. This directory lists and describes all the newspapers and periodicals of the world, by trade classification. So, for example, you could find the names of all the magazines published on the subject of Camping, Caravanning and Rambling – which would be a source of considerable information on companies, markets and products in that sphere of interest.

Directory of British Assocations published by CBD Research Publications, 154 High Street, Beckenham, Kent BR3 1EA. Lists and describes all the trade and other associations in the UK by field of interest, each of which is an invaluable source of information in their respective fields.

Analysing the competition

The following are some of the areas that you should cover in this section of your business plan:

Description of competitors

Identify those businesses which are or will be competing with you. If the number is few, list them by name. If there are many, then describe the group without naming them individually ('47 charter fishing boat operators'). List any expected or potential competitors.

Jonathon Woodrow, a 25-year-old fine arts graduate who took part in a Cranfield enterprise programme, prepared the following preliminary analysis of the likely competitors to his company, Mainframe:

Framing outlets (franchised). A company called Fastframe, based in the Newcastle area, was established in 1983. They adapted an American approach to the system, which incorporates the latest picture-framing machinery in workshops attached to the picture shops. They have now established nearly 50 outlets across the country, through a franchise operation which has a combined turnover of £4 million a year. None is based in the Greater London Area.

In 1984 a company called The Frame Factory was set up in North London. They have established 10 shops in Cambridge, Nottingham and secondary locations in Islington, Hampstead and London suburbs such as Streatham and Hornsey. Some of these have been set up under a recent franchise operation.

Framing outlets (multi-location). In 1984 Frame Express was set up in Wimbledon, London. This company closely followed the Fastframe approach (they were originally registered as Fastaframe). They have now established eight shops in central and south-east London.

A slightly different approach to fast framing has been introduced recently by a company called Fix-a-Frame. They operate two shops, in Old Brompton Road SW5 and Swiss Cottage in north-west London. Here, customers are invited to do part of the work on their frames themselves, under supervision. This obviously cuts costs, and may appeal to certain customers, but for many people cost is acceptable if the service is good, and very often time is the important factor.

Independent shops. By far the majority of picture framing outlets in London are operated as independent shops providing a local service on a small scale. They offer diverse services which frequently take weeks to achieve, and are considerably more expensive than most fast framing shops. This is because they incur greater labour charges and do not enjoy the benefits of bulk purchase, due to their comparatively low volume of trade.

Local competition. A survey of the area around Holborn confirms that there are no frame shops comparable to the Mainframe operation for at least a one-mile radius. There are three shops offering a framing service within a short walking distance of the site, of which only one treats framing as the primary activity. These are not seen as direct competition, as they appear to be aiming at a local domestic market, which is not the principal Mainframe target.

Size of competitors

Determine the assets and sales volume of the major competitors. Will you be competing against firms whose size is similar to yours or will you be competing against giant corporations? If assets and sales volume cannot be determined, try to find other indications of size, such as number of employees, number of branches etc.

The proprietor of 'Scoops', a proposed pick'n'mix sweet shop, got something of a shock researching his market while on an enterprise programme at Cranfield. He found out from Companies House that the small shop in Bath he proposed to emulate was owned by a multinational food company, and was not a one-man band as he thought. Further research revealed that this multinational planned a chain of franchised outlets if the Bath shop was a success.

His original strategy was to open a similar shop in another town and then perhaps grow slowly over five more years. This new information on his competitive environment confirmed that the market was very attractive, but forced him to adopt a different strategy on premises. He couldn't hope to match a franchisee-resourced chain head on, so he went for a shop-in-shop approach. This meant he could open new outlets at least as fast as his competitor, but use even less capital. His first concession in Hamley's in Birmingham was successful, leading to three more outlets in his first year of operations – a rate of growth he could not have sustained adopting his original strategy.

Profitability of competitors

Try to determine how profitable the business is for those companies already in the field. Which firms are making money? Losing money? How much?

Operating methods

For each of the major competitors, try to determine the relevant operating methods. For example, what pricing strategy does each firm use? Others, besides price, that you may consider are:

- Quality of product and/or service
- Hours of operation: ability of personnel
- Servicing, warranties, and packaging

- Methods of selling: distribution channels
- Credit terms: volume discounts
- Location: advertising and promotion
- Reputation of company and/or principals
- Inventory levels.

Many of the above items will not be relevant to all businesses. Location will not be relevant, perhaps, to a telephone answering service. On the other hand, there are many items that are not listed above which may be very relevant to your business. In the motor trade, trade-in value and styling may be as relevant as the price. So it is very important for you to determine the relevant characteristics on which you will do your research.

Summary of analysis of competitors

After you have completed your research it is useful to summarise your findings in tabular form, such as the table shown on page 82. Keep in mind that the characteristics listed are for illustration only. You must decide the relevant characteristics that will go into your own table.

When the table is complete, analyse the information contained in it to reach your conclusions. Is there a correlation between the methods of operation and other characteristics, and the size and/or profitability of the competitors? A thoughtful analysis is essential because there may be many patterns shown. For instance, you may find that all the profitable companies are large, and all the unprofitable companies are small. That would be an easy pattern to spot (and an important one, as well) because it involves only two factors, profitability and size. However, it is more common that success and failure correlate with a number of factors that are not always so easy to discern, even when your findings are summarised on one page.

Looking for patterns is not the only type of analysis that is needed. You may find that a company is very successful, even though its characteristics are completely different from the other profitable firms. What factors apparently contribute to its success? Or you may find that a company is failing despite the fact that its operational characteristics are similar to those of the profitable firms. Can you identify the reason?

Once you have reached conclusions about the competition, relate them to your business. What is the competitive situation in the market? Is everyone making money and expanding, or is it a dog-eat-dog situation? Are your competitors likely to be much larger than you? If so, what effect will this have? Are there some operating methods that appear critical to success in this market? If so, will you be able to operate in the necessary fashion? Are there operating methods or characteristics not being widely used in the market which you think have merit? If so, why are they not found at present? Is it because they have been overlooked, or because they have problems which you have not foreseen?

The above are some of the questions that you will want to address. You will probably have many others. The important thing, though, is for you to decide the general outlook for your business. At this point in your research, does it appear that you will be able to compete successfully in this market? Do you now feel that you know what it will take in order to compete successfully? If you can answer these two questions to your satisfaction, you have probably done an adequate job of research.

Brighton Furniture Co Ltd

Despite the fact that there are over 100 furniture dealers in Brighton, the bulk of the new flats and town house developments get their furniture packages from only six firms. In my market research I found that from 80-99 per cent (depending on who you talk to) of the 'packages' were sold by those six firms. The firms are identified by name in the table on page 80.

Product characteristics

To get information on the products sold by each of the firms, I talked to eight developers who had selected one or more of the six firms to provide a furniture package for their units. I also talked to 23 individuals who had purchased a package for their premises from one of the six firms. In general, the purchasers felt that their furniture was performing about as they had expected. The one exception was that buyers of the Apartment Furniture Co all felt that the quality was not as good as they had been led to believe.

A summary of other characteristics for each company is presented in the table on page 80. Based upon these findings, I have divided the six into three groups, and labelled them as follows:

High quality, high price. The only firm in this category is Rattan Imports, which sells only Rattan furniture. As one would expect, its sales are to the more expensive developments.

Moderate price, high quality. Again, only one firm, Georgian Furniture, is in this category. The bulk of its sales were made in developments where one-bedroom units cost from £75,000–£100,000, although it did get the contract for one more expensive building.

Low price, varying quality. Four of the six firms appear to be competing in the lower end of the package deal market. Three of the four sell 'casual' furniture, and the fourth sells bamboo furniture. Overall, there is not much difference in warranty and delivery service, but there is some variation in price (from a low of £4200 to a high of £5100) and upkeep (Apartment Furniture Co and Bamboo Things Ltd appear to require less maintenance than the other two). There is, however, a wide disparity between the firms in trade-in value.

Bamboo Things furniture holds its value much better than the other firms' products, almost 2.5 times better than AAA and Apartment Furniture.

Company characteristics

By talking to four of the six firms (the other two refused) and by researching various published sources, I was able to prepare the table on page 80. Some characteristics that bear mentioning are:

- All six firms use in-house sales people rather than manufacturers' representatives.
- There does not seem to be any particular correlation between performance and the number of years in business.
- Although the sales of the two firms that concentrate on the higher priced furniture are relatively small, their profits as a percentage of sales are very high.
- The two firms that manufacture their own furniture have the lowest profits as a percentage of sales.

Analysis of competition

Based upon the data gathered, the following analysis of the competition seems reasonable:

- The high price, high quality segment of market seems the most profitable. There is only one competitor; the firm has been in existence only two years and sales are already over £500,000 a year; profit/sales is running at 25 per cent; and the firm is not quite as aggressive as it could be since it requires full payment on delivery.
- The moderate price, high quality segment of the market also seems to have good potential since there is only one firm presently in the market. On the negative side, this firm has been operating a year longer than Rattan Imports and seems to be more aggressive than Rattan (as shown by its lower profit/sales ratio and its more liberal credit policy), yet its total sales ratio may be low because of some inefficiencies on the company's part.
- The lower priced segment of the market seems to be very competitive. Of particular concern is the fact that two of the firms manufacture their own furniture. AAA Furniture is the leader in terms of both price and sales, and yet its profits and those of the other manufacturer, Apartment Furniture, seem very low.

  It seems likely that both these companies are willing to accept low profits because they are making the bulk of their money manufacturing. This fact is important because it means that they could even afford to sell at a cheaper price and make money, whereas I have to make a profit on the retail sales.

  The fact that Condo Supplies is able to remain profitable in the face of this competition is due to the company's years in business, and the reputation for quality and service that it has cultivated with the big developers. A new firm, such as mine, would be at the mercy of the

Company information

Competitors' names	Sales	Profits	Year started	Credit terms	Sales people/ Reps	Manufacturer
Condo Supplies Co	750,000	125,000	1975	50% deposit	Sales people	No
Georgian Furniture	300,000	60,000	1980	50% deposit	Sales people	No
AAA Furniture Inc	1,250,000	75,000	1978	COD	Sales people	Yes
Rattan Imports Inc	500,000	125,000	1981	COD	Sales people	No
Bamboo Things Ltd	600,000	150,000	1980	50% deposit	Sales people	No
Apartment Furniture Co	400,000	10,000	1977	COD	Sales people	Yes

manufacturers since I do not have the reputation of the firms such as Condo Supplies, nor the unique product such as Bamboo Things Ltd.

Based on this, I conclude that I have neither the unique line nor the reputation to compete successfully in the lower priced end of the market. However, I feel that I can upgrade my quality sufficiently to enter the moderate price, high quality or the high price, high quality segments. Of the two, the high price segment seems most likely since Rattan Imports is not as aggressive as is Georgian Furniture; also, the high price segment seems to be larger and faster growing than the moderate price segment.

Worksheet for Assignment 5: Competitors

1. List and briefly describe the companies with whom you will be competing directly.
2. Analyse their size, profitability and operating methods, as far as you can.
3. What are their relative strengths and weaknesses compared both with each other and with your business?
4. What, in the light of this competitive analysis, do you believe to be the critical factors for success in your business sector?
5. What is unique about your business that makes it stand out from the competition?

Suggested further reading
Competitive Strategy, Michael E Porter, The Free Press, 1980.

Analysis of competition

Name	Assets	Profits	Sales	Quality	Credit terms	Location	Price	Customer service	Inventory levels	Direct sale or wholesale

Conclusions: Key factors for success in your industry are:

Assignment 6
A Plan for Market Research

It is unlikely that you will already have the answers to all the important questions concerning your market-place.

The purpose of the market research element of the workbook is to ensure you have sufficient information on customers, competitors and markets so that your market entry or expansion strategy is at least on the target, if not the bull's eye itself. In other words, enough people want to buy what you want to sell at a price that will give you a viable business. If you miss the target completely, you may not have the resources for a second shot.

Before embarking on your market research you should first set clear and precise objectives, rather than just setting out to find interesting 'general' information about the market. For example, if you are planning to open a shop selling to young fashion-conscious women, your research objective could be: to find out how many women aged 18–28, in the income range £8000+ pa live or work within two miles of your chosen shop position.

The next step is to see if someone else has the answers already. Market research conjures up images of people with clipboards accosting you in the street – and you might well have to do that. But much of the information you need will already be published, so some of your market research activity, at least, can be done in a comfortable chair in a good library. For instance, the official Census of Population will supply you with demographic data on size, age and sex of the local populace, and there is a wealth of government and other published statistics to enable you to work out the size and shape of the market nationwide and the expenditure per head of population.

This type of research is called desk research and it is well worth doing. Listed below are some of the most relevant directories and other information sources. Please note that any prices shown are indicative rather than actual, as they are changed from time to time.

Market research information sources

The A-Z of UK Marketing Data, published by Euromonitor Publications Ltd, provides basic market data for several hundred UK markets from adhesives to zip fasteners, by product area, market size, production, imports, exports, the main brands, their market share and the market forecast. A good glimpse at a wide range of markets.

Acorn, a classification of residential neighbourhoods, is published by CACl Market Analysis (59–62 High Holborn, London WC1V 6DX; 01-404 0834). Every postcode area in the UK is described by one of nearly 40 Acorn codes, ranging from run-down terraces, to farm cottages, to high status areas with few or no children – the ubiquitous Dinkys (Double income, no kids).

Knowing these characteristics it is possible to work out whether a given area is likely to want your products or services. For example, if you were considering opening a shop in Bedford (near Cranfield), this Acorn-based site report would help to assess its potential:

> Bedford is a thriving town within commuting distance of London, and the figures support that picture. For instance, 14 per cent more of Bedford's population go to work by car than is true of the country as a whole. Nearly 22 per cent of Bedford households have two or more cars – that's 40 per cent above the national average. Similarly, the percentage of owner-occupiers is 19% per cent above the national average, and the number of council house tenants is a third below. In terms of Acorn categories, Bedford scores well above the rest of the UK on all types of modern private housing estates, from the low cost to the relatively expensive. The town also has more young families and less unemployment than average.

Annual Abstract of Statistics, published by the Central Statistical Office, is the basic source of all UK statistics. Figures are given for each of the preceding 10 years, so trends can be recognised.

BBC Data Enquiry Service, Room 3, The Langham, The British Broadcasting Corporation, Portland Place, London W1A 1AA; 01-927 4338. This is a personal information service drawing on the worldwide resources of the BBC. It is an inexpensive and speedy way of checking facts and drawing on a statistical data bank which covers people, products, countries and events. The service could tell you the price of a pint of milk in 1951 or the current state of the Dutch economy. *Ad hoc* enquiries can cost as little as £5 or an annual subscription of £100.

British Rate and Data, updated monthly. Whatever you are interested in, it is almost certain to have a specialised paper or journal which will be an important source of market data. BRAD lists all newspapers and periodicals in the UK and the Irish Republic which carry advertising, and gives their frequency and circulation volume, price, executives' names, advertising rates and readership classification.

Business Monitors are the medium through which the government publishes the business statistics it collects from over 20,000 UK firms. They are the primary and very often the only source of detailed information on the sectors they cover. The Monitors can help business people by indicating trends and tracing the progress of 4000 individual products, manufactured by firms in 160 industries. Monitors can also be used to rate your business performance against that of your industry and to measure the efficiency of different parts of your business.

The Monitors are published in three main series. The *Production Monitors* are published monthly, quarterly and annually. The quarterly is probably the most useful, with comprehensive yet up-to-date information. The *Service and Distribution Monitors* cover the retail market, the instalment credit business, the motor trade, catering and allied trades and the computer service industry, among others. Finally, there are *Miscellaneous Monitors* covering such topics as shipping, insurance, import/export ratios for industry, acquisitions and mergers of industrial and commercial companies, cinemas and tourism.

The Annual Census of Production Monitors cover virtually every sector of industry, and include data on total purchases, total sales, stocks, work in progress, capital expenditure, employment, wages and salaries. They include analysis of costs and outputs, of establishments by size, of full- and part-time employees by sex, and of employment, net capital expenditure and net output by region.

You can use the information – particularly that from the size analysis table – to establish such ratios as gross output per head, net output per head, net to gross output, and wages and salaries to net output. With these as a base, you can compare the performance of your own business with the average for firms of similar size and with that for your particular industry as a whole. For example, you can discover your share of the market and compare employment figures, increases in sales, and so on.

Most of the libraries listed on page 88 will have a selection of the *Business Monitor* series. Individual Monitors can be bought from HMSO Books, PO Box 569, London SE1 9NH. They are all individually priced.

Guide to Official Statistics is the main guide to all government produced statistics, including *ad hoc* reports. It is published by HMSO at £18.50. However, a brief free guide is available from the Press and Information Service, Central Statistical Office, Great George Street, London SW1 3AQ.

Key Note Publications. Publishers of the same name at 28–42 Banner Street, London EC1Y 8QE; 01-253 3006, produce concise briefs on various sectors of the UK economy.

Each *Key Note* contains a detailed examination of the structure of an industry, its distribution network and its major companies; an in-depth analysis of the market, covering products by volume and value, market shares, foreign trade and an appraisal of trends within the market; a review of recent developments in the industry, highlighting new product development, corporate development and legislation; a financial analysis of named major companies, providing data and ratios over a three-year period together with a corporate appraisal for the industry, including estimates from Key Note's own database and authoritative trade sources. There is a very useful appendix detailing further sources of information – recent press articles, other reports and journals.

Over 100 market sectors are covered, including such areas as adhesives, after-dinner drinks, bicycles, butchers, commercial leasing, health foods, road haulage, public houses, travel agents and women's magazines. Each *Key Note* costs about £100.

Kelly's Business Directory published by Kelly's Directories, Windsor Court, East Grinstead House, East Grinstead, West Sussex RH19 1XB, has an alphabetical list of manufacturers, merchants, wholesalers and firms, together with their trade descriptions, addresses, telephone and telex numbers. In addition, entries are listed by trade classification. A section lists British importers under the goods they import. Exporters are listed by the products they export and the continent and countries in which they sell. The directory covers 90,000 UK firms classified under 10,000 trade, product or service headings.

Key British Enterprises published by Dun and Bradstreet Ltd, 26–32 Clifton Street, London EC2P 2LY; 01-247 4377, contains information on 20,000 UK companies that between them are responsible for 90 per cent of industrial expenditure. *KBE* is very useful for identifying sales prospects or confirming addresses, monitoring competitors and customers or finding new suppliers. As well as giving the names, addresses, telephone and telex numbers of the main office of each company, it gives branch addresses, products indexed by SIC (Standard Industrial Classification) code, sales turnover (UK and overseas), directors' names and responsibilities, shareholders, capital structure, trade names and number of employees.

By using the directory you can quickly establish the size of business you are dealing with and what other products or services they offer. It is very often important to know the size of a firm if, for example, your products are confined to certain types of business. A bookkeeping service is unlikely to interest a large company with several hundred employees; they would have their own accounts department.

Kompass is published in two volumes in association with the Confederation of British Industry. Volume I is indexed by product or service to help to find suppliers, and indicating whether they are manufacturers, wholesalers or distributors. It can be very useful on certain occasions to be able to bypass a wholesaler and get to the manufacturer direct. Volume II gives basic company information on the 30,000 suppliers identified from Volume I. It includes the address, telephone and telex numbers, bankers, directors, office hours and the number of employees.

Office of Population, Censuses and Surveys produces demographic statistics for each county in England and Wales from the census. These provide data not only on total populations in each area, but also on occupations, economic groups etc. Similar reports for Scottish and Northern Irish regions are also available. There is a reference library at OPCS, St Catherine House, 10 Kingsway, London WC2B 6JP; 01-242 0262. More information and answers to general enquiries on these reports are also available from this number on extensions 2009 and 2013.

Overseas Trade Statistics published by the Department of Trade and Industry, provide a monthly statement of UK imports and exports by volume and value for each product group and individual country. The Bill of Entry Services, operated by HM Customs and Excise, Portcullis House, 17 Victoria Avenue, Southend-on-Sea, Essex SS2 6AL; 0702 49421, extension 310, will provide more detailed information for a fee.

Published Data on European Industrial Markets, published by Industrial Aids Ltd, 14 Buckingham Palace Road, London SW1W 0QP; 01-828 5036. Part I lists over 1900 market research reports available for purchase at prices from as low as £10 up to several thousand pounds. Although the directory is entitled 'industrial' the interpretation is fairly wide. It covers consumer goods as markets for industrial products, and financial and economic planning studies, where they are considered of possible interest to industry. This could be a relatively inexpensive way of finding out about a distant market-place. Part II is a guide to other sources of information on European industrial markets, including international statistical and individual country sources.

Reports Index, Business Surveys Ltd, PO Box 21, Dorking, Surrey RH5 4EE; 0306 87857. This is an index to reports in every field published and available for sale. Its sources include government publications, HMSO and other market research organisers, educational establishments, the EEC, industrial and financial companies. Cost: £94 per annum.

The Retail Directory, published by Newman Books, 48 Poland Street, London W1V 4PP; 01-439 0335, gives details of all UK department stores and private shops. It lists the names of executives and merchandise buyers as well as addresses and telephone numbers, early closing days etc. It also covers multiple shops, co-operative societies, supermarkets and many other retail outlets. If you plan to sell to shops, this is a useful starting point, with around 1305 department stores and large shops and 4821 multiple shop firms and variety stores listed in 1346 pages. If you are already selling retail, this directory could help you to expand your prospect list quickly. The directory also identifies high turnover outlets for main product ranges. There is a useful survey showing retail activities on each major shopping street in the country. It gives the name and nature of the retail business in each street.

A separate volume contains shop surveys for the Greater London area, with 27,830 shops listed by name, street number and trade. The head offices of 1130 multiples are given, as are 233 surveys showing what sort of shops are in any area. This can also be used for giving sales people useful contacts within their territory.

Finding the information

Now that you have an idea of the considerable mass of data that is available about companies, their products and markets, the next problem is to track it down. Fortunately, many of the directories and publications are kept in reference sections of major libraries up and down the country. If you know exactly what information you want, then your problem is confined to finding a library or information service that has that information.

Specialist libraries

Apart from your local library, which may well have all the answers you require, there are hundreds of specialist libraries concentrated in government departments, major industrial companies, trade organisations, research centres and academic institutes. Two useful publications that will help you to find out about these are listed below.

ASLIB Economic and Business Information Group Membership Directory, published by the group and available from the London Business School Library, Sussex Place, Regent's Park, London NW1 4SA; 01-262 5050. This provides a list of over 300 specialist business libraries throughout the country and gives a very useful guide to their area of specialist interest.

Guide to Government Departments and Other Libraries. The 25th edition, published in 1982, is the latest and is available from the Science Reference Library, 25 Southampton Buildings, Chancery Lane, London WC2A 1AW, price £9. As the title indicates, this book concentrates on libraries in government departments and agencies, and particularly avoids duplicating the ground covered by the *ASLIB Directory*. The entries are arranged by subject, supplemented by an alphabetical index of the libraries, their locations, telephone numbers and opening hours.

Not all the libraries covered in these directories are open to the public for casual visits. However, many will let you use their reference facilities by appointment.

If you are in or near London you can visit or contact: the Science Reference and Information Service, Department of British Library, 25 Southampton Buildings, Chancery Lane, London WC2A 1AW; 01-405 8721, extension 3344 or 3345. Patent enquiries: extension 3350, telex 266959. This is the national library for modern science and technology, for patents, trade marks and designs. It has the most comprehensive reference section of this type of literature in western Europe. If you have no adequate library close at hand a visit here could save you trips to several libraries. It should also be able to provide you with answers if most other places cannot do so.

The library's resources are formidable. It has 25,000 different journals, with issues back to 1960 on open shelves and the rest quickly available; 85,000 books and pamphlets and over 20 million patents. It has a worldwide collection of journals on trade marks, together with books on law and design. Most of the major UK and European reports are held, as are trade literature and around 1000 abstracting periodicals.

The services are equally extensive. It is open from Monday to Friday, 09.30 to 13.00. You can visit without prior arrangement or a reader's ticket. Telephone requests for information, including the checking of references, are accepted. Once at the library, staff are available to help you to find items and to answer general queries. Scientific staff are also on hand for specialised enquiries. There is even a linguist service to help you inspect material written in a foreign language, although for this service you must make an appointment.

The Business Information Service of the Science Reference Library; 01-323 7464, was set up in January 1981, primarily to support the activities of other business and industrial libraries. However, it will help individual users as much as possible. Staff here can extract reference information quickly, advise on the use of business literature and suggest other organisations to contact. For extensive research you will have to call in person, but they can let you know if a visit would be worthwhile.

Information services

In addition to the many excellent libraries up and down the country there is an increasing number of organisations that will do the searching for you. The benefits to you are twofold: professionals search out the data and can alert you to sources that you may not have thought of; they also save you time, not just the time you would spend searching. If you are far from a good business reference library you may have a considerable and expensive journey to make.

Organisations in the field include:

Industrial Aids Ltd, enquiry service at 14 Buckingham Palace Road, London SW1W 0QP; 01-828 5036, telex 918666 CREGON G. This service is geared to supply commercial and technical information, such as who makes what/where/how much. Who is company A's agent in country X? Where are custom manufacturing sources? Details are given of company financial data, affiliations, product literature, consumption patterns, end users, prices, discounts and trading terms, as well as new legislation and standards. The cost is £40 per enquiry, excluding VAT.

The Marketing Shop, 18 Kingly Court, Kingly Street, London W1R 5LE; 01-434 2761, telex 262284. This organisation provides a wide range of marketing services but its information service is perhaps the most useful facility for small businesses. It can provide data on practically any topic, either using its own library or outside sources, and will also monitor the media for information on companies' products or markets. The charge is £40 per hour for *ad hoc* work. The more usual arrangement is for customers to take a block of hours to be used over the year. Block fees start at around £500 which entitles you to about 15 hours' research time.

Warwick Statistics Service, University of Warwick Library, Coventry CV4 7AI; 0203 523251, telex 31406. This service offers a range of commercial and economic information based on published sources including international statistics, both official and non-official, market research, periodicals, reports, directories, company reports and on-line services. The service can be particularly helpful to a small business, with information on market size and share, locating particular types of company and finding out about them, trading recent articles on a particular product or process, on consumer expenditure data, imports and exports, economic conditions, price trends, advertising expenditure and production of sales figures.

The service will also undertake analysis of the data in question, and provide a written report on their desk research. In general, enquiries are dealt with on the telephone, telex or by post; however, personal visits are welcome. If you telephone beforehand, documents can be assembled for you to look at.

Annual subscribers to the service pay £330 for 10 hours' search time and publication. Occasional users of the service can get information or research assistance on an *ad hoc* basis at a cost of £50 per hour pro rata, with a minimum charge of £15. All in all, it is very good value.

Field research

In some cases, the answers to your questions won't exist in published form since no one else will have been interested enough to have researched and published the data – for example, how many young people pass a particular shop front each day. There you will need to undertake some original market research. This activity, often called field research, means you (or people you employ) have to go out and ask the questions yourself.

Sampling

The first problem you will face is to decide how many people to include in your survey.

Suppose you wanted to find out how many shoppers passed down Kensington High Street every year, and how much they each spent. Clearly, you could not stand in the High Street and interview every single person for a whole year. By the time you got the answer it would be too late and the cost too high.

Equally obviously, if you asked the first person you saw how much they spent, and then multiplied it by the number of people passing in a day, and then multiplied that by the days in a year, your answer would be too inaccurate to be of use.

So, somewhere between the whole population and one person lies a satisfactory number of people to include in your 'sample'. In practice, between 100 and 200 completed replies will usually give a reliable guide. Within limits, the larger your sample size the more 'accurate' the emerging picture will be. But there are sharp diseconomies. Doubling the sample size, if it is already large, will not improve the accuracy by a significant amount – perhaps a few per cent only – but it will double the cost of the survey.

You must also make sure that the sample taken is representative of all the groups of people that you are interested in finding out about. For example, men and women, high income and low income, commuters and non-commuters.

The questionnaire

This is the research technique most commonly used by small and new ventures. Questionnaires can be answered in face-to-face interviews, over the telephone or by post. Here are some rules to observe when designing a questionnaire:

1. Keep the number of questions to a minimum. People don't have unlimited time and you run the danger of sidetracking the objectives if you ask too many questions.
2. Keep the questions simple. Answers should either be yes/no/don't know, or offer at least four choices. For example, if the question is, 'How interested are you in going to the theatre?' the respondent should be asked to answer, 'very, fairly, not very, or not at all'. This helps you to assess what proportion of respondents would almost definitely take advantage of a new product or service and what proportion just might.
3. Make sure the respondent really understands the question – so avoid ambiguity.
4. Avoid opinions, stick to asking for factual answers.
5. Make sure you have a cut-out question to eliminate 'unsuitable' respondents, for example, non-decision makers.
6. Make sure you have an identifying question so you can be sure that you have an appropriate cross-section of respondents.

Observations

Sometimes it isn't necessary to carry out full-scale surveys. You have probably come across people with counters monitoring the traffic or how many cars have driven over rubber strips in the road. These are 'observation research techniques', which count the number of people doing a particular thing. An application of this for a new business is to count the number of customers or delivery vans coming and going to a competitor's premises. This information could give you some idea as to his size, if that was not available from other sources.

Who can help?

There are a large number of specialist market research companies and you can obtain a list from the Market Research Society, 15 Belgrave Square, London SW1X 8PF; 01-235 4709. They will advise you how best to conduct your research, devise tests and questionnaires, and analyse the results.

Professional market research is a sophisticated operation and it isn't cheap; conducting interviews with 100 shoppers, for instance, could cost you £1000. There are ways to get less expensive help, though. Students on business study courses have to carry out projects as part of their course work and tutors are keen to ensure that this project resembles real life as closely as possible, so you may be able to get them to undertake some of your market research for a modest fee. Contact the marketing department of a local college or polytechnic. One college has set up a full-time business in this field and its services are professionally recognised, at about one-third of the market price. Contact: Scanmark, Buckinghamshire College of Higher Education, Newland Park, Chalfont St Giles, Bucks HP8 4AD; 02407 4441.

Sharing the costs

Designing a questionnaire and interviewing a balanced sample of respondents is an expensive and time-consuming business. One way round the problem is to use an 'omnibus' survey, which asks questions on behalf of a number of different clients, so cutting the costs. Several market research firms carry out market research on a regular basis, so all you have to do is tell them the questions you want to ask. Most surveys are conducted face-to-face, but some are done by telephone. There are general surveys covering a national representative sample, and specialist surveys for those interested in only a particular market sector, for example, young people, motorists, mothers with 0-2 year olds etc.

General Omnibus Operators are run by firms whose names will already be familiar to you – Gallup, MORI and NOP, for instance. Their charges include an entry fee, usually payable once only, and a charge per question. These sums are between £100-£200 and £150-£400 respectively, depending on the sample size.

Specialist surveys are carried out less frequently than general surveys – monthly, quarterly or less often.

If you're interested in things medical or pharmaceutical you can choose between Martin-Hamblin Research's *Mediline* (a sample of 400 GPs); costs £90 entry fee to question 200 users of health products (£200 a question).

Travel and Tourism Research offer a *Travel Agents Omnibus Survey* (200 agents, minimum fee £500). Produce Studies' *Omnifarm* is a panel of 1000 farmers (minimum fee £900), and *Omnicar* from Sample Surveys investigates the attitudes and behaviour of 1000 motorists (£100 entry fee, £260 per question). Research Surveys of Great Britain also offer a *Motoring Omnibus* (1000 motorists, entry fee £150, £250 per question) while Public Attitude Surveys look at the beer drinking habits of 1680 adults each month (around £320 per question).

Firms wi ᵗh products or services tailored to particular age groups might like to ᵒntact Carrick James who do monthly surveys of children and teenagers mothers with different-aged children and, occasionally, grandmothers as well (£190 entry fee, around £145–£380 per question depending on the sample size). Harris Research conduct a *Young Persons Omnibus* (1500 people between 12 and 24, £150 entry fee, £285–£385 per question) and Research Surveys of Great Britain, a *Baby Omnibus* (not a sample of highly articulate infants but of 700 mothers with 0-2 year olds, entry fee £150, £260 per question).

If you're operating from Scotland or Ulster, or wish to test-market in these areas, System Three offers a monthly omnibus of 1000 Scots (£130 entry fee, £140 per question) and Ulster Marketing Services, a Northern Irish survey (1100 adults, no entry fee and from £310 per question, which buys you a full report with commentary).

Business to Business. Those wanting to question other businesses can use *Key Directors Omnibus* from Audience Selection (a quarterly survey of 600 decision-makers from the top 10 per cent of British business in three separate categories: 200 managing directors/chief executives, 200 financial directors, 200 sales and marketing directors; no entry fee, £275 to question 200). With *Telebus*, from Market Research Enterprises (a quarterly telephone survey of 1200 business people, mainly from small- or medium-sized firms), you can opt for different categories: office managers, computer executives, marketing personnel etc (£200 entry fee, £250 per question). *Business Line* from Business Decisions asks questions of 2000 small businesses (no entry fee, around £550 per question for 2000, £275 per 1000).

Addresses

Audience Selection
10–14 Macklin Street, London WC2B 5NF
01-404 5015

British Market Research Bureau Ltd
53 The Mall, Ealing, London W5 3TE
01-567 3060

Business Decisions
25 Wellington Street, London WC2E 7DW
01-379 7458

Carrick James Market Research
11 Great Marlborough Street, London W1
01-734 7171

Harris Research Centre
Holbrooke House, Holbrooke Place, 34–38 Hill Rise, Richmond,
Surrey TW10 7UA
01-948 5011

Market & Opinion Research International
32 Old Queen Street, London SW1H 9HP
01-222 0232

Market Research Enterprises Ltd
Doric House, 22 Charing Cross Road,
London WC2H 0JU
01-836 8962

Marplan Ltd
Bridgewater House, 5–13 Great Suffolk Street, London SE1 0NS
01-928 1200

Martin-Hamblin Research
Mulberry House, 36 Smith Square, London SW1P 3HL
01-222 8181

MAS Survey Research Ltd
25 Wellington Street, London WC2E 7DW
01-240 2861

NOP Market Research Ltd
Tower House, Southampton Street, London WC2E 7HN
01-836 1511

Produce Studies Ltd
Northcroft House, West Street, Newbury, Berkshire RG13 1HD
0795 23778

Public Attitudes Surveys Research Ltd
PO Box 91, Rye Park House, London Road, High Wycombe,
Bucks HP11 1EF
0494 32771

Research Surveys of Great Britain Ltd
Research Centre, West Gate, London W5 1EL
01-997 5555

RBL
PO Box 203, Green Bank, London E1 9PA
01-488 1366

Sample Surveys Ltd
82 Bishops Bridge Road, London W2 6BB
01-229 1403

Social Surveys (Gallup Poll) Ltd
202 Finchley Road, London NW3 6BL
01-794 0461

Survey Force Ltd
Algarve House, 140 Borden Lane, Sittingbourne, Kent ME9 8HR
0795 23778

System Three Scotland
16 York Place, Edinburgh EH1 3EP
031-566 9462

Taylor Nelson Medical
44–46 Upper High Street, Epsom, Surrey KT17 4QS
Epsom 29688

Travel & Tourism Research
Lector Court, 151–153 Farringdon Road, London EC1R 3AD
01-837 1797

Ulster Marketing Surveys Ltd
115 University Street, Belfast BT7 1HP
0232 231060

Character (Self-assembly Furniture) Ltd

Market research sampling strategy and details

Sample size: 100–200

96

The desk research has identified the most likely customers as being homemakers in the higher social groups. The age ranges are likely to be 25–44 (male) and 25–34 (female).

Since it is hoped that certain items within the product range will interest younger flat-sharing but ambitious singles, eg dismountable shelving systems, and older comfortably settled couples, eg garden furniture, the views of these groups are also of interest.

Saturday canvassing will take place at indoor shopping centres or in supermarket or garden centre car parks.

Weekday canvassing will be aimed at lunch breaks – the period between 12.00 and 2.00pm.

Research results (number of respondents: 75)

Due to the number of questions in the questionnaire and the time required to fill them out, railway stations were eventually used as interview locations.

Interview at Cheltenham Spa Station took place on 22 and 23 October 1987, and 35 interviews were conducted at Euston Station (London) on Saturday 31 October. See Table 1 for sub-groupings of respondents.

The survey showed clearly that people were aware of the existence of self-assembly furniture (SAF); only one person out of the 75 interviewed (a sub-group F member) professed to never having thought about it. Overwhelmingly this awareness was related to shelves (which were home-made rather than self-assembled) and fited kitchen or bedroom furniture. Individual respondents did mention an array of other items of SAF of which they knew or had had some personal experience, for example, a rocking chair, a filing cabinet, and two claimed to know of SA chests-of-drawers.

The question of seasonality showed that only six respondents opted for seasons, four for spring and two for winter. The other 69 said that they would buy furniture at any time.

Table 1. Sub-groupings of respondents

Age group	Group 1: A,B	Group 2: C1	Group 3: C2, D,E
18–24 No married/partner Sex		8 **C** 2 7M + 1F	11 **F** none 6M + 5F
25–44 No married/partner Sex	10 **A** 7 7M + 3F	21 **D** 17 14M + 7F	12 **G** 8 4M + 8F
Over 45 No married/partner Sex	4 **B** 2 1M + 3F	7 **E** 5 4M +3F	2 **H** 1 2F
Total in group	14	36	25

Notes:

43 respondents were male (M)
32 respondents were female (F)

A–H sub-group letters used as headings for tables following.

Social groups were allocated on the basis of occupations and newspapers read. Home ownership was then applied to help to clarify a subject's socio-economic grouping.

All values given in the following tables are percentages, rounded to the nearest 1%.

Since only two of the group 3 respondents were over 45 years of age, the terms *one* or *both* are applied to describe their views rather than the use of statistics which would be meaningless.

Table 2. Main reasons for buying SAF

	A	B	C	D	E	F	G	H
Price	80	–	50	71	29	100	83	one
Convenience	40	–	–	48	29	–	17	–
Cash & carry	–	25	–	43	57	27	17	–
Hobby	–	–	–	–	–	18	–	one
Fits own space	–	–	–	19	–	–	–	–

Notes:

Price came out in almost all interested groups as being of primary importance (overall 86% of ABs, 60% of C1s and 88% of group 3 C2s and below gave it as the main reason for buying SAF). Also of significance, as shown by the tables, were convenience and cash and carry, principally the facility to be able to take the furniture away at the time of purchase, rather than having to wait for its delivery.

In general the 'best off' seemed to want 'good' furniture that would last and they were prepared to pay for it. All group 1 over 45s said they disliked SAF in general.

Many people, of all social groups, tended to regard SAF as 'cheap and cheerful'. The main criticisms were as shown in Table 3.

Table 3. Main criticisms of SAF

	A	B	C	D	E	F	G	H
Fiddly to build	20	–	75	–	–	73	50	one
Difficult to build	60	–	–	19	57	55	33	–
Poor finish/quality & looks cheap	20	50	–	19	–	9	33	–
Not sturdy	–	–	–	48	29	–	–	one
No tools/not handy	20	50	25	10	–	–	–	–
Poor instructions	–	–	–	10	–	–	–	–
Bits missing	–	–	–	29	–	9	33	–
No time	–	–	25	10	–	18	–	–

Notes:

The most common criticisms were that SAF was fiddly or difficult to put together and that it lacked sturdiness. A significant proportion of all groups thought that it looked cheap. 50% of the highest social group of over 45s couldn't really be bothered with it and a significant number of respondents complained of bits missing from flatpacks.

Table 4. SAF: Buying patterns past and future

	A	B	C	D	E	F	G	H
Had bought SAF in the past	80	50	75	100	86	55	66	one
Would buy SAF in the future	80	50	100	91	43	100	83	one

Notes:

Most of those who had bought SAF in the past would buy again. Younger respondents in general were more likely to entertain the idea of buying SAF in the future anyway. In spite of their reservations about sturdiness, quality etc, most who had bought in the past would do so again.

Table 5. Types of SAF bought in the past

	A	B	C	D	E	F	G	H
Shelves	40	50	–	57	29	18	–	–
*Kitchen units	40	–	25	57	–	45	50	one
*Bedroom units	20	–	25	–	–	18	33	–
Beds	20	–	13	9	–	27	50	–
Garden furniture	40	50	–	9	–	–	–	one
Wardrobes	–	–	13	19	–	–	33	–

Notes:

*A positive response in either of these categories could have meant anything from a complete fitted kitchen or bedroom, down to a wall-mounted cupboard or self-assembled sink unit. In view of my own interests when preparing the questionnaire I did not think it necessary to be more specific. My own opinion is that fully fitted installations are usually carried out by contractors.

Other 'one offs' bought included an SA filing cabinet which took 'hours to put together', a dining room suite (table and chairs) and a Habitat drawing table. However, most commonly bought were kitchen and bedroom units and shelves, all as reflected by the previous Mintel research.

Table 6. Buying intentions, next 12 months

	A	B	C	D	E	F	G	H
Unlikely	10	100	–	43	71	18	33	–
Possibly	70	–	50	29	29	64	17	both
Intending to	20	–	50	29	–	18	50	–

Notes:

Significant numbers, especially of the younger age groups in each category, are intending to or considering buying SAF in the next 12 months.

Table 7. What SAF is it likely to be?

	A	B	C	D	E	F	G	H
Shelves	40	50	25	19	29	27	33	-
Kitchen units	40	-	25	29	-	54	17	-
Bedroom units	20	-	25	29	-	18	17	both
Beds	10	-	-	10	-	-	-	-
Wardrobes	20	-	13	19	-	18	-	-
Garden furniture	-	50	13	10	-	-	17	-

Notes:

Shelves, kitchen and bedroom units featured highest in the list along with garden furniture, especially for older people and higher social groups.

Table 8. Positive response to system evolution ideas

	A	B	C	D	E	F	G	H
Cot to playpen to climbing frame	60	100	50	71	57	64	50	-
Bed to bunks etc	80	50	50	57	57	55	50	-
Shelving/dividers system	80	100	75	81	71	82	83	both

Notes:

The shelf system idea was most liked but, as shown, the other ideas were also well received.

Table 9. Would ease of taking apart be a useful feature?

	A	B	C	D	E	F	G	H
Yes	50	50	75	81	43	73	83	both

Notes:

This seems to be an attractive feature (when specifically put and the advantages explained) especially with younger groups likely to want to move flat/house. Older people might find its value in being able more easily to carry things up and down stairs and, for example, to get chairs of the right height. Comments such as, 'if it doesn't fall apart first' or 'not likely, when it's so difficult to put together in the first place', also reflected people's general attitude towards the perceived sturdiness of SAF.

Table 10. Who bought the SAF?

	A	B	C	D	E	F	G	H
Male	60	50	50	29	43	27	100	–
Female	20	–	25	–	–	27	–	one
Both	20	50	25	71	57	45	–	one

Notes:

This shows that singly or in partnerships men still tend to be the buyers, but among couples the shared decision is common. Only in the third group (25-44 year age group) did the man still appear to dominate the choice.

Table 11(a). Styles and woods people like

	A	B	C	D	E	F	G	H
Painted	20	–	–	14	–	17	–	–
Stained	20	50	25	29	–	17	50	one
Natural	80	50	75	71	100	83	50	one

Table 11(b)

	A	B	C	D	E	F	G	H
Pine	60	50	50	57	57	66	–	–
Teak	–	50	25	10	57	33	–	–
Mahogany	20	50	25	47	29	33	–	–
Oak	40	25	–	47	–	17	–	–
Beech	20	–	–	–	–	–	–	–
Walnut	–	25	–	–	–	–	–	–
Light wood	40	–	–	10	36	–	–	–
Dark wood	–	–	75	10	36	–	–	–
Depends	40	–	25	10	18	17	100	both

Notes:

Most people of all social groups preferred natural wood finishes. Pine and mahogany fared best, in that order, with teak third. Oak also fared well in terms of numbers, especially in the higher social groups, but many respondents said that the type of wood they liked depended on where it was to be displayed.

Conclusions

Although the sample analysed was relatively small, compared to the Mintel samples, it is still clear that the target groups to be aimed at mainly include the under 44s of both sexes in all groups, in agreement with the earlier desk research.

Clear intentions to buy furniture within the next 12 months were expressed by a significant proportion of those sampled, which is reassuring, as was the overall response to the furniture system evolution ideas, with most respondents showing the greatest interest in the shelving system. Without showing people actual products it will not be possible to gauge their sincerest opinions. Not surprisingly, the most likely purchases were shelves, kitchen and bedroom units.

The largest proportion of respondents in all categories preferred natural wood. Pine was the most popular, but mahogany, teak and oak also were popular in that order. Pine was clearly preferred by the younger group 3s.

Many people are still to be convinced that sturdiness, simplicity of construction and quality can be synonymous with SAF. If it is possible to offer these qualities and make it known, along with the benefits, for example, of being able to disassemble the furniture easily and to build chairs to your own desired height etc, then it should be possible to stimulate a wider interest in SAF.

The areas to concentrate on appear to be shelves, kitchen and bedroom units and garden furniture, but if the benefits offered in connection with chair structures and shelf, cot and bed evolution systems are made clear by 'aggressive' promotion, there seems no reason why these systems too wouldn't do well.

Self-assembly furniture (SAF)
Market Research Questionnaire

INSTRUCTIONS Fill in as many boxes as apply in the following way:
✓ = Yes,   X = No,   ? = Maybe, or leave Blank.
Fill in a short statement when required.

Q

1. Date ☐ `/ /88`

2. Time ☐

3. Which do you live in?

    Flat ☐

    House ☐

4. Is it your own home? ☐

5. What types of SAF have you seen?

    Shelves

    Bed

    Kitchen units

Bedroom units ☐

Wardrobe ☐

Chest-of-drawers ☐

Cupboard ☐

Garden furniture ☐

Other (State which) _____

_____

6. Have you, or anyone in your home ever bought SAF?

☐ If X go to Q9.

7. What type of SAF was it?

Shelves ☐

Bed ☐

Kitchen units ☐

Bedroom units ☐

Wardrobe ☐

Chest-of-drawers ☐

Cupboard ☐

Garden furniture ☐

Other (State which) _____

_____

8. Who in your household bought the SAF?

I did ☐

Partner ☐

We did ☐

Son/Daughter ☐

Other (State which) _____

_____

9. Would you consider buying SAF in the future?

☐

10. What do you like about SAF?

Price ☐

Hobby ☐

Can be taken apart ☐

Convenience of transport ☐

Cash and carry ☐

Nothing ☐

Other (State which) _____

_____

11. What *don't* you like about SAF?

Price ☐

Difficult to assemble ☐

Fiddly to assemble ☐

I've no tools ☐

No time/energy ☐

Not sturdy ☐

Appearance (Explain) _____

_____

Other (State which) _____

Stained ☐

Natural ☐

15. If natural, what sort of wood?

Pine ☐
Teak
Mahogany
Ash
Light colour
Dark colour
Don't know

Other (State which) _____

_____

12. Would ease of taking apart be an attractive feature? ☐

13. Which newspapers do you normally have at home?

Local (Advertiser) ☐
Local (News)
Sun
Star
Mirror
Express
Mail
Telegraph
Guardian
Independent
Times
Observer

Other (State which) _____

_____

16. What is the likelihood of your buying furniture within the next 12 months?

Unlikely ☐
Possibly
Intending to

17. What furniture is it likely to be when you do buy?

Shelves ☐
Bed
Kitchen units
Bedroom units
Wardrobe

14. What finishes in wooden furniture do you like?

Painted ☐

Chest-of-drawers ☐

Cupboard ☐

Garden furniture ☐

Other (State which) _____

_____

21. Marital status ☐
           Single

22. What sort of work do you do?

(State)_____

_____

18. When are you most likely to buy furniture?

Spring ☐

Summer ☐

Autumn ☐

Winter ☐

Any time ☐

23. Which is your age group?

18–24 ☐

25–29 ☐

30–39 ☐

40–44 ☐

45–59 ☐

>60 ☐

19. Would you consider buying SAF *because* it could be developed into other items of furniture, even if this meant later additional purchases?

eg Cot to playpen to climbing frame ☐

eg Single bed to double bed *or* bunks *or* four poster ☐

eg A shelf system that would grow with additional purchases ☐

Other system suggestions (State)

_____

_____

24. If you have children which age group are they in?

Up to 10 ☐

11–18 ☐

20. Sex M/F (ring which applies)

106

Worksheet for Assignment 6: A plan for market research

1. What information do you currently have on customers, competitors, markets etc?
2. What information do you still need to find, and why specifically do you need it?
3. What desk research will you have to carry out to answer this question?
4. What field research will you have to carry out?
5. How much time and money will be needed to carry out this market research?
6. Who will be responsible for each element of the research?
7. When will all the key market research information be available?

Suggested further reading

The Market Research Process, 2nd edition, Margaret Crimp, Prentice Hall, 1985.

The Small Business Guide, 3rd edition, Colin Barrow, BBC Publications, 1988.

Sampling site			Form No.

Q
1. / / 88 1
2. 2
3. 3
4
4. 5
5. 6
7
8
9
10
11
12
13
14
6. 15
7. 16
17
18
19
20
21
22
23
24

Q
8. 25
26
27
28
29
30
9. 31
10. 32
33
34
35
36
37
38
11. 39
40
41
42
43
44
45
46
12. 47

Q
13. 48
49
50
51
52
53
54
55
56
57
58
59
60
14. 61
62
63
15. 64
65
66
67
68
69
70
71
16. 72
73
74

Q
17. 75
76
77
78
79
80
81
82
83
18. 84
85
86
87
88
89
90
91
92
20. M/F 93
21. 94
22. 95
23. 96
97
98
99
100
101
102
24. 103

19.

Phase 3
Competitive Business Strategy

Introduction

The data you have begun to collect should enable you to formulate a competitive business strategy. This will involve explaining exactly how you intend to satisfy your target customers, with the products or service you will provide, in the face of competition.

Keith Musto, a silver medallist in the 1964 Tokyo Olympics, explains how he developed a winning strategy for Musto Ltd, his sailmaking business.

'In 1971 we recognised that the boat clothing market was wide open. Most of it was being made by clothing manufacturers who were not sailors. We felt we could turn our sewing machines from making sails to making clothes, faster than they could learn to sail. We knew what was needed to improve clothing design to make sailors perform better. A warm, dry sailor is a safer sailor.'

Musto now has a range of six designs to clothe any mariner, from windsurfer to round-the-world yachtsman. He uses the best synthetic materials to keep the wearer comfortable in a three-layer system, which consists of, 'Good underwear that sucks the moisture from the skin like blotting paper; then a middle layer using fibres to trap as much warm air as possible; and a protective outer layer to keep the storms out.'

His clothing has been endorsed by leading yachtsmen. But the biggest accolade came when the company won a Duke of Edinburgh's Design Award for its latest outfit. The British and Spanish lifeboatmen will wear jackets and trousers based on this design, which was rigorously tested by the RAF's Medical Research Centre at Farnborough.

'We were a long way ahead of our competitors in those tests', says Musto. 'The Spaniards knew the RNLI and the RAF were very thorough and were happy to follow on.'

You have at your disposal a 'mix' of ingredients which, according to how they are used, can produce different end results. There will obviously have to be an internal consistency in your actions. For example, a high quality image, supported by a prestige location and sophisticated advertising, is hardly consistent with a very low price and untidy staff.

The principal elements of this 'marketing mix', as it is frequently called, are the *product* or service you have to sell, the *price* you propose to charge, the *promotion* you will use to communicate your message, and the *place* you will operate from or the distribution channels you will use (ie where do your customers have to be for you to get at them?).

You may find when you come to tackle the assignments in this phase that you have to collect more data. This is not unusual – indeed, gathering information is a continuous activity in a healthy business. Unfortunately, this healthy search for additional data can lead to some confusion as to how eventually to formulate strategy.

The strategic framework shown opposite should put the whole strategic process clearly in view and help you to formulate a clear course of action.

Strategic framework

The foundation of this process is a clear statement of the mission of your venture, your objectives and the geographic limits you have set yourself, at least for the time being. These issues were addressed in the first assignment and until they are satisfactorily resolved no meaningful strategy can be evolved.

Market research data is then gathered on customers, competitors and the business environment, for example, to confirm that your original perception of your product or service is valid. More than likely this research will lead you to modify your product in line with this more comprehensive appreciation of customer needs. You may also decide to concentrate on certain specific customer groups. Information on competitors' prices, promotional methods and location/distribution channels should then be available to help you to decide how to compete.

No business can operate without paying some regard to the wider economic environment in which it operates. So a business plan must pay attention to factors such as:

- The state of the economy and how growth and recession are likely to affect such areas as sales, for example.
- Any legislative constraints or opportunities. One Cranfield enterprise programme participant's entire business purpose was founded to exploit recent laws requiring builders and developers to eliminate asbestos from existing properties. His business was to advise them how to do so.
- Any social trends that may have an impact on market size or consumer choice. For example, the increasing number of single parent families may be bad news at one level, but it's an opportunity for builders of starter unit housing. And the increasing trend of wives returning to work is good news for convenience food sales and restaurants.

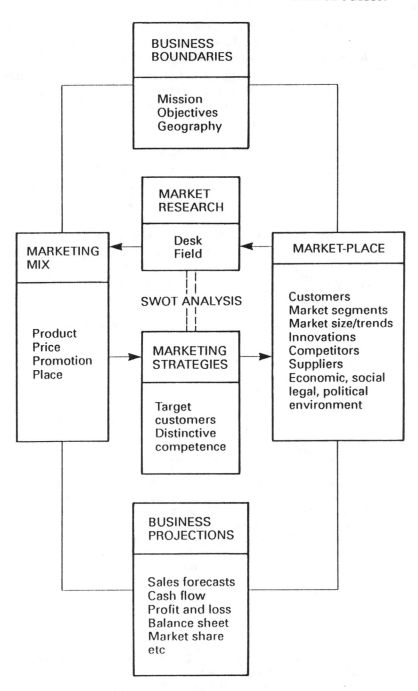

- Any political pressures for or against your business sector. An example is the small private landlord who, virtually made extinct by various Rent Acts, was revived by the 1987 Housing Bill, signalled in the Conservative Manifesto prior to the election. The same manifesto announced the proposed introduction of a 'poll tax', which by virtue of its difficulty to administer, has provided a major opportunity for computer and software houses to market 'solutions' to local councils.

The process by which all this data is examined is called the SWOT Analysis: strengths, weaknesses, opportunities and threats. Its purpose is to allow you to develop a strategy using areas in which you are more able than the competition to meet the needs of particular target customer groups.

The final element in this strategic framework is a projection of the likely financial outcome of your strategic decisions. The outcome should, of course, coincide with your starting objectives.

An example of a competitive business strategy for a recent Cranfield enterprise programme participant is set out below.

Competitive business strategy for the Total Yoghurt Company

We plan to specialise in retailing Frozen Yoghurt, a product similar in appearance and consistency to icecream. There all similarities end as our product is far lower in terms of calories, and is designed as a healthy and delicious snack that can be eaten throughout the year. There will be a variety of flavours, ranging from cappuccino to mandarin orange, complemented by a choice of optional toppings from fresh fruit to chocolate chip – the yoghurt and topping combined will be known as 'Frogurt'.

We are aiming at three primary segments:

- The youth market, aged 6 to 18, who will make up a small portion of our customer base. They will prefer simple flavours with sweet toppings.
- The 18 to 35 age range, who, Euromonitors' 'Healthy Food and Healthy Eating Report' provides irrefutable evidence, combine a rapidly increasing health awareness level with a growing demand for convenience foods and confectionery items. This segment will be the most adventurous, preferring fruity flavours with fresh fruit toppings.
- The final segment is the 35+ age range, who, although even more health conscious than earlier groups and with the highest disposable income, are less likely to be product innovators than either of the previous groups.

There is strong evidence that all three of these segments are already 'heavy' yoghurt users and the overall market has grown from £90 million in 1980 to £281 million in 1987.

There is also evidence that much of this rapid growth can be attributed to new product innovations such as Frogurt. In 1980 fruit yoghurt claimed

93 per cent of the market but by 1986 this had shrunk to 50 per cent, with children's natural, whole milk, set type, long life and very low fat yoghurt claiming the balance.

Our objectives are:

Short term – 6 months to 2 years

- To have our first frozen yoghurt outlet up and running successfully.
- To have developed a sound base of expertise upon which to build a substantial enterprise.

Long term – 2 to 7 years

- To have 3–6 retail outlets up and running, owned and managed by the Total Yoghurt Company Ltd.
- To have 15 franchised outlets opened up.
- To make Frogurt a household name.

There are currently six retailers of frozen yoghurt in London:

The Garden Store, Holborn – health food/fruit shop.
Natural Dividends, Trocadero – healthy fast foods.
Onion, Holborn – sandwich bar.
Selfridges, Oxford Street – food hall.
Harrods, Knightsbridge – food hall.
Healthy Eats, Victoria Station – healthy fast foods.

The above outlets exist only as indirect competition to the Frogurt outlet for two reasons:

- Frogurt will specialise in frozen yoghurt, whereas the above treat it as an additional product.
- Frogurt will be started in catchment areas largely unaffected by the above outlets' market-place.

Competition will arise in the form of icecream outlets and vans, although Frogurt is not to be seen as an icecream substitute but rather as a completely different concept of a soft-serve, low calorie, healthy and original snack.

Marketing strategy (product, price, promotion and place)

One of our policies is to use yoghurt with natural ingredients. The frozen yoghurt mix used in the production of Frogurt contains non-fat milk solids, honey, fructose, no preservatives, no fat or salt and only natural colouring from beetroot and elderberries. The natural, healthy and low calorie features of Frogurt will appeal to all consumers whose health awareness levels have been or are increasing. The delicious flavours and toppings coupled with the product's originality are features which will appeal to consumers regardless of their health interest.

Product. There will be five yoghurt flavours to choose from. This range of flavours will change from day to day. Complementing this variety will be 7–10 different types of topping which will be a fixed range. The on-the-spot nature of the manufacturing process means that once the outlet has closed and the machines have been cleaned out, a new flavour may be used the following day. The flavours available from our suppliers can be found in the appendix (not included here). The proposed toppings are as follows:

- fruit salad
- crushed nut
- chocolate chip
- mini marshmallow
- raisins or sultanas
- granola
- smarties

The product will be served in small, medium and large sizes.

Price. Prices will vary according to the size of yoghurt serving. There will be one price charged for any of the toppings which will be optional. Given a cost of approximately 20 pence for a 3.5 ounce serving and an expected gross profit margin of 75 per cent, the average price of the product is 80 pence. The expected prices per serving are as follows:

small	60p
medium	80p
large	100p
toppings	20p

Further analysis of costings, projections and competitors' prices are shown in the appendix.

Promotion. These techniques and ideas are being evaluated for the promotional aspect of the business:

(a) A large emphasis will be placed on hygiene at each outlet and this will be portrayed by specifically designed fixtures and fittings.
(b) All the positive aspects of the product will be conveyed to the consumer in point of sale displays making specific claims about the product, eg, non-fat. Emotive wording will be used to create the healthy image as well as to show the product's originality.
(c) All toppings will be attractively displayed within the service counter, either on a bed of ice for perishable types or in vertical compartments for non-perishables.
(d) Initially, a flyer distributed to passers-by will serve to inform consumers about the outlet, the product and its benefits. It will also serve to entice customers to try the product for free on production of the flyer – this will entail a tiny serving.
(e) Editorial coverage in local and tourist press will be sought to announce the opening of each outlet, and to describe the product, its price and the free tastings available.

Place

Location. The targeted market segments described in Section 2 show that an area must be picked to ensure the presence of the particular age groups and socio-economic classes required to form the customer base. The three main areas chosen as possible locations are:

- busy shopping centres
- underground and mainline train stations
- international airports

These three possible locations each have two vital characteristics:

- High levels of consumer traffic. This means that awareness levels concerning the outlet and its product will rise quickly, as well as serving to ensure high turnover levels.
- Captive markets. None of the above targeted locations will be exposed to the elements. This will ensure the protection of turnover levels from the harmful effects of seasonality, as well as creating the scenario for the 'impulse buy' to take place as consumers window-shop or await trains and flights.

Premises. The premises will have an area of approximately 300 square feet with as large a frontage as possible – approximately 15 feet. The frontage will act as the counter over which customers will be served; this will be transparent so that customers can see what toppings are available. There will be no seating facilities provided as the frontage will face directly on to the main concourse of the shopping centre, station or airport. The premises must have a water supply to enable washing facilities to be installed and an electricity supply to run the machinery and lighting. Fixtures and fittings will be designed to convey an exciting, new and healthy image.

The 300 square feet will be divided into:

- A service area containing washing, storage, staff and refrigeration facilities.
- The area exposed to the general public containing the machines involved in the on-the-spot manufacturing process, fixtures and fittings, the toppings and counter unit and the staff themselves.

In the next three assignments we will look closer at the key elements of marketing strategy.

Assignment 7
Pricing

The most frequent mistake made when setting a selling price for the first time is to pitch it too low. This mistake can occur either through failing to understand all the costs associated with making and marketing your product, or through yielding to the temptation to undercut the competition at the outset. Both these errors usually lead to fatal results, so in preparing your business plan you should guard against them.

These are the important issues to consider when setting your selling price.

Costs

Make sure you have established *all* the costs you are likely to incur in making or marketing your product. Don't just rely on a 'guess' or 'common sense' – get several firm quotations, preferably in writing, for every major bought-in item. Don't fall into the trap of believing that if you will initially be working from home, you will have no additional costs. Your phone bill will rise (or you will fail!), the heating will be on all day and you'll need somewhere to file all your paperwork.

One potential entrepreneur, when challenged as to why there were no motoring expenses budgeted for in his business plan, blandly replied he already owned his car and paid its running expenses. It had not occurred to him that the average personal miles done per annum are 12,000 and for the self-employed businessman that rises to nearly 30,000. Similarly, his insurance could nearly double as a business user, his service charges and petrol would increase directly with the increased mileage, and the expected useful life of his car would be reduced from six years to three. The net effect of this was to wipe out his projections for a modest profit in the first year and push his break-even out to the second year.

Also make sure you analyse the effect of changes in turnover on your costs. This can be by breaking down your costs into direct and indirect (see Assignment 15 for an explanation of break-even analysis, as this area is sometimes referred to).

Consumer perceptions

Another consideration when setting your prices is the perception of the value of your product or service to the customer. His opinion of value may have little or no relation to the cost, and he may be ignorant of the price charged by the competition, especially if the product or service is a new one. One example of extremes in setting new prices was provided when Ferguson launched its pocket colour TV at Christmas 1987. Ferguson concluded that their younger and more affluent customers wanted a television that could be a constant companion – and that they would be prepared to part with £250 for that privilege. Casio entered the market with a rival product a few weeks later at around half that price! Presumably Casio's selling price will cover their costs, so Ferguson's price must be mainly based on their view of the customer's perception of value.

Competition

The misconception that new and small firms can undercut established competitors is usually based on ignorance of the true costs of a product or service, such as in the example given above; a misunderstanding of the meaning and characteristics of overheads; and a failure to appreciate that 'unit' costs fall in proportion to experience. This last point is easy to appreciate if you compare the time needed to perform a task for the first time with that when you are much more experienced (eg, changing a fuse, replacing a hoover bag etc).

The overhead argument usually runs like this: 'They (the competition) are big, have a plush office in Mayfair, and lots of overpaid marketing executives spending the company's money on expense account lunches, and I don't. *Ergo* I must be able to undercut them.' The errors with this type of argument are, first, that the Mayfair office, far from being an 'overhead' in the derogatory sense of the word, is actually a fast appreciating asset, perhaps even generating more profit than the company's main products (department stores, restaurants and hotels typically fit into this category). Second, the marketing executives may be paid more than the entrepreneur, but if they don't deliver a constant stream of new products and new strategies they'll be replaced with people who can.

Clearly, you have to take account of what your competitors charge, but remember price is the easiest element of the marketing mix for an established company to vary. They could follow you down the price curve, forcing you into bankruptcy, far more easily than you could capture their customers with a lower price.

Elasticity of demand

Economic theory suggests that, all others things being equal, the lower the price the greater the demand. Unfortunately (or perhaps not!), the demand for all goods and services is not uniformly elastic – that is, the rate of change of price versus demand is not similarly elastic. Some products are actually price inelastic. For example, Jaguar and Rolls-Royce would be unlikely to sell any more cars if they knocked 5 per cent off the price – indeed by losing 'snob' value they might even sell less. So, if they dropped their price they would simply lower profits. However, people will quite happily cross town to save 5p in the £1 on fresh vegetables and meat.

So setting your price calls for some appreciation of the relative elasticity of the goods and services you are selling.

Company policy

The overall image that you try to portray in the market-place will also influence the prices you charge.

However, within that policy there will be the option of high pricing to skim the market and lower pricing to penetrate. Skim pricing is often adopted with new products, with little or no competition and aimed at affluent 'innovators'. These people will pay more to be the trend setters for a new product. Once the innovators have been creamed off the market, the price can be dropped to penetrate to 'lower' layers of demand.

The danger with this strategy is that high prices attract the interest of new competitors, who see a good profit waiting to be made.

Opening up with a low price can allow you to capture a high market share initially, and it may discourage competitors. This was the strategy adopted by Dragon Lock, Cranfield enterprise programme participants (the executive puzzle makers), when they launched their new product. Their product was easy to copy and impossible to patent, so they chose a low price as a strategy to discourage competitors and to swallow up the market quickly.

Business conditions

Obviously, the overall conditions in the market-place will have a bearing on your pricing policy. In 'boom' conditions, where products are virtually being rationed, the overall level of prices for some products could be expected to rise disproportionately. In 1985–87 house prices, for example, rose sharply ahead of general price inflation. During the recession of the mid-1970s house prices fell, in real terms.

Seasonal factors can also contribute to changes in the general level of prices. A turkey, for example, costs a lot less on the afternoon of Christmas Eve than it does at the start of Christmas week.

Channels of distribution

Your selling price will have to accommodate the mark-ups prevailing in your industry. For example, in the furniture business a shop may expect to set a selling price of double that charged by its supplier. This margin is intended to cover their costs and hopefully make a profit. So, if your market research indicates that customers will pay £100 for a product bought from a shop, you, as the manufacturer selling to a shop, would only be able to charge £50.

Capacity

Your capacity to 'produce' your product or service, bearing in mind market conditions, will also influence the price you set. Typically, a new venture has limited capacity at the start. A valid entry strategy could be to price so high as to just fill your capacity, rather than so low as to swamp you. A housewife who started a home ironing service learnt this lesson on pricing policy to her cost. She priced her service at £2.50 per hour's ironing, in line with competition, but as she only had 20 hours a week to sell she rapidly ran out of time. It took six months to get her price up to £5 an hour and her demand down to 20 hours a week. Then she was able to recruit some assistance and had a high enough margin to pay some outworkers and make a margin herself.

Bigmack Health Food

The average mark-up by Bigmack Health Food Co's (BHFC) competition is 300 per cent. This mark-up is necessitated by the high cost of their locations and the cost of personnel. After careful analysis of the costs involved, BHFC has determined that it could use a mark-up of only 200 per cent and still make a sizeable profit. BHFC will be able to do this because:

- Its location costs will be one-third less than that of the major competition. This is due to our ability to focus on a specific market segment made up of aware customers, who are prepared to buy from smaller, secondary locations (our market research has confirmed this view).
- The employee costs of BHFC will be only 20 per cent of the costs incurred by the competition. This is due to the fact that BHFC's customers will be almost entirely long-time health food devotees who

will not need assistance or advice to select their purchases. The competition, on the other hand, has a constant stream of people who are novice health food consumers or who are not interested in health food but want to purchase, on a one-time basis, a particular product. These types of people require a lot of advice and instruction and thus several employees must be working at all times.

The company will sell on credit to several health food restaurants. It will require that they pay COD for the initial order but will allow a 'net 30 day' account thereafter if their credit is adequate. All other sales will be on a cash basis.

Policy

BHFC will adopt an introductory pricing policy using a 300 per cent mark-up, offering selective new customer discounts for the first month that will bring the mark-up down to 200 per cent.

In this way we can test the market at the higher price level and only come down if we have to, and so achieve the optimum revenue.

Worksheet for Assignment 7: Pricing

1. List all the costs you are likely to incur in making or marketing your product.
2. Refer forward to Assignment 14 and then calculate the fixed and variable costs associated with your product.
3. Using the costs as calculated above and your profit objective, calculate the optimal price you should charge.
4. What price do your competitors charge?
5. Are any of your possible market segments less price sensitive than others?
6. Does your answer to question 5 lead you to believe that there is an opportunity for a differentiated pricing policy for each market segment – so enhancing profits?

Suggested further reading
Effective Marketing Management, Ch 4, Getting the Price Right, Martin Christopher, Malcolm MacDonald, The Open University, 1986.
Competitive Strategy, Michael E Porter, Macmillan, 1980.
Successful Business Strategy, Len Hardy, Kogan Page, 1987.

Assignment 8
Advertising and Promotion

In this section of your business plan, you should discuss your planned advertising and promotion programme. A major decision is to choose a method of advertising that will reach most of your customers for the least cost. Advertising is a specialised field and, whenever possible, you should use an advertising agency, but if you're like most small businesses, advertising agencies and market research firms are often not affordable. Contact several local agencies to discuss your needs and resources before deciding that you are unable to afford them. You will learn a lot about the business of advertising in the process, and you may even alter your own plans.

Promotion/advertising checklist

Advertising is to some extent an intangible activity, although the bills for it are certainly not. The answers to these five questions should underpin the advertising and promotional aspects of your business plan:

- What do you want to happen?
- How much is that worth?
- What message will make it happen?
- What media should be used?
- How will results be checked?

What are your advertising objectives?

There is no point in informing, educating or pre-selling unless it leads to the opportunity in a significant number of instances for a sale to result. So what does the potential customer have to do to enable you to make these sales? Do you want him to visit your showroom, to phone you, to write to your office, return a card, or send an order in the post? Do you expect him to have an immediate need to which you want him to respond now, or is it that you want him to remember you at some future date when he has a need for whatever it is you are selling?

   The more you are able to identify a specific response in terms of orders, visits, phone calls or requests for literature, the better your promotional effort will be tailored to achieve your objective, and the more clearly you will be able to assess the effectiveness of your promotion and its cost versus its yield.

The more some particular promotional expenditure cannot be identified with a specific objective but is, for example, to 'improve your image' or 'to keep your name in front of the public', then the more likely it is to be an ineffective way of spending your money. Prospective financiers will be particularly wary of advertising expenditure detailed in your business plan, as this money, once spent, is gone forever, unlike expenditure on cars, equipment or even stocks, which have at least some recoverable element.

How much is it worth to achieve your objective?

Once you know what you want a particular promotional activity to achieve, it becomes a little easier to provide for it in your business plan. In practice, four methods are most commonly used, and they each have their merits, with the exception of the first.

'The 'What can we afford?' approach has its roots in the total misconception of promotional activity, which implies that advertising is an extravagance. When times are good, surplus cash is spent on advertising and when times are bad this budget is the first to be cut back. In fact, all the evidence points to the success of businesses that increase promotional spending during a recession, usually at the expense of their meaner competitors.

The 'percentage of sales' method very often comes from the experience of the entrepreneur or his colleagues, or from historical budgets. So, if a business spent 10 per cent of sales last year, they will plan to spend 10 per cent in the next, particularly if things went well. This method at least has some logic and provides a good starting point for preparing the overall budget.

'Let's match the competitors' becomes a particularly important criterion when they step up their promotional activity. Usually this will result either in your losing sales or feeling threatened. In either case you will want to retaliate, and increasing or varying your promotion is an obvious choice.

The 'cost/benefit' approach comes into its own when you have clear and specific promotional goals and an experience base to build on. If you have spare capacity in your factory or want to sell more out of your shop, you can work out what the 'benefit' of those extra sales is worth.

Suppose a £1000 advertisement is expected to generate 100 enquiries for our product. If our experience tells us that on average 10 per cent of enquiries result in orders, and our profit margin is £200 per product, then we can expect an extra £2000 profit. That 'benefit' is much greater than the £1000 cost of the advertisement, so it seems a worthwhile investment.

In practice, you should use all of these last three methods to decide how much to spend on promoting your products.

What message will help to achieve the objectives?

To answer this question you must look at your business and its products from the customer's standpoint and be able to answer the hypothetical question, 'Why should I buy your product?' It is better to consider the answer in two stages.

1. 'Why should I buy your *product*?'
   The answer is provided naturally by the analysis of factors which affect choice. The analysis of buying motives or satisfactions is an essential foundation of promotional strategy.

2. 'Why should I buy *your* product?'
   The only logical and satisfactory answer is: 'Because it is different'. The difference can arise in two ways:

   We – the sellers – are different.
   Establish your particular niche.

   It – the product – is different.
   Each product should have a unique selling point, based on fact.

Your promotional message must be built around these factors and must consist of facts about the company and about the product.

The stress here is on the word 'fact' and while there may be many types of fact surrounding you and your products, your customers are only interested in two: the facts which influence their buying decisions, and the ways in which your business and its products stand out from the competition.

These facts must be translated into benefits. There is an assumption sometimes that everyone buys for obvious, logical reasons only, when we all know of innumerable examples showing this is not so. Does a woman only buy a new dress when the old one is worn out? Do bosses have desks that are bigger than their subordinates' because they have more papers to put on them?

Having decided on the objective and identified the message, now choose the most effective method of delivering your message.

What media should you use?

Not all methods of communication have an equal impact. We are much more likely to be favourably influenced if a trusted and respected friend recommends a product or service to us, rather than a door-to-door salesman.

In practice, most new businesses should concentrate their advertising and promotional activity on the following:

Press advertising

From your market research you should have a clear idea of who your potential customers are – in terms of socio-economic classification, for example. Your business plan should detail the media you plan to use.

These associations and publications can provide information that will help you with press advertising (addresses at end of section):

Advertising Association
Institute of Practitioners in Advertising
Regional Newspapers Advertising Bureau
British Rate and Data (BRAD)
Benn's Media Directory

Leaflets/brochures and letters

This is the most practical way for a new business to communicate with its potential customers. It has the merits of being relatively inexpensive, simple and quick to put into operation, it can be concentrated into any geographic area, it can be mailed or distributed by hand and finally, it is easy to monitor results.

> Oliver and Tom Vaughan, then aged 20 and 18 respectively, launched Juliana's the 'socially acceptable' discotheque company in 1967 on the back of a £200 bank loan. They got equipment and vans on hire purchase and used the cash to buy the top 50 singles.
>
> They combed the social columns of the quality press for names and sent out persuasive letters. Their message was: 'Our service is the most expensive, but we do everything – move the furniture, stay till the last guest has gone and clear up afterwards.' It was these promotional ideas in their business plan that persuaded the bank manager to back them – and it worked.
>
> Within 10 years they were millionaires, and by 1983 Juliana's was listed on the Stock Exchange. Turnover is now £10 million, they employ 300 people, have 110 discotheque contracts and own five clubs, including Raffles in Hong Kong.

These organisations can provide information that will help you with leaflets and brochures:

British Direct Marketing Association

Institute of Marketing
British List Brokers Association
Astro Mailing

Public relations

This is about presenting yourself and your business in a favourable light to your various 'publics' – at little or no cost. It is also a more influential method of communication than general advertising – people believe editorials.

> Chantal Coady, who founded Rococo, the unique King's Road confectioners in 1981, was 22 when she wrote the business plan that secured her £25,000 start-up capital. The cornerstone of her strategy to reach an early break-even point lay in a carefully developed public relations campaign. By injecting fashion into chocolates and their packaging, she opened up the avenue to press coverage in such magazines as *Vogue, Harpers & Queen*, and the colour supplements. She managed to get over £40,000 worth of column inches of space for the cost of a few postage stamps. This not only ensured a sound launch for her venture but led to a contract from Jasper Conran to provide boxes of chocolates to coordinate with his spring collection.

To be successful, a press release needs to get attention immediately and be quick and easy to digest. Studying and copying the style of the particular journals (or other media) you want your press release to appear in can make publication more likely.

- *Layout.* The press release should be typed on a single sheet of A4. Use double spacing and wide margins to make the text both more readable and easy to edit. Head it boldly 'Press Release' or 'News Release' and date it.
- *Headline.* This must persuade the editor to read on. If it doesn't attract interest, it will be quickly 'spiked'. Editors are looking for topicality, originality, personality and, sometimes, humour.
- *Introductory paragraph.* This should be interesting and succinct and should summarise the whole story – it might be the only piece published.
- *Subsequent paragraphs.* These should expand and colour the details in the opening pragraph. Most stories can be told in a maximum of three or four paragraphs. Editors are always looking for fillers, so short releases have the best chance of getting published.
- *Contact.* List at the end of the release the name and telephone number of a contact for further information.
- *Style.* Use simple language, short sentences and avoid technical jargon

(except for very specialised technical magazines).

- *Photographs.* They must be black and white, reasonably sized and well captioned. Don't staple them to the release (photographs with holes are unpublishable).
- *Follow-up.* Sometimes a follow-up phone call to see if editors intend to use the release can be useful – but you must use your judgement on how often to do so.

Find out the name of the editor or relevant writer/reporter and address the envelope to him or her personally.

These publications can provide you with information on press releases, as can some organisations listed earlier:

Hollis Press and Public Relations Annual
Contact House, Lower Hampton Road, Sudbury-on-Thames, Surrey

PRADS Media List
Press Information and Mailing Services, Faber Court, 4 St John's Place, London EC1

Exhibitions

As a means of gathering market research data on competitors, exhibitions are extremely valuable. They are also a useful way of establishing the acceptability of your product or service quickly and relatively inexpensively, and so provide a convincing argument in support of your case for financial backing.

> Equinox, a designer furniture company, took part in their first national exhibition while on a Cranfield enterprise programme. The cost of their stand at Earls Court was £1200. They secured £5000 of new orders, which just recovered their exhibition costs, but more importantly they got 40 contacts to follow up. These eventually resulted in 10 further long-term customers. This whole process took two months, and transformed Equinox from the drawing board to being a bankable proposition.

There are hundreds of exhibitions to choose from. You can find a list of those forthcoming in the monthly publication *Exhibition Bulletin*, available directly from the publisher: The London Bureau, 266/272 Kirkdale, Sydenham, London SE26 4RZ; 01-778 2288, cost £4 per single issue, £27 annual subscription. *EB* also contains lists of useful related services, such as transport hire, stand designers and staffing agencies.

These organisations and publications are referred to in the 'What media should we use?' section:

Advertising Association, Abford House, 15 Wilton Road, London SW1Y 1NJ; 01-828 2772. Formed in 1926, its aim is to promote awareness of the effectiveness of the different types of advertising.

British Direct Marketing Association, 1 New Oxford Street, London WC1A 1NQ; 01-242 2254. Its members include direct mail houses who prepare and market lists of prospective customers.

Institute of Marketing, Moor Hall, Cookham, Maidenhead, Berkshire SL6 9HQ; 06285 24922. The main professional marketing association, which includes advertising agencies.

Institute of Practitioners in Advertising (IPA), 44 Belgrave Square, London SW1X 8QS; 01-235 7020. The majority of reputable advertising agents belong to the IPA, who can provide a list of members and guidelines for choosing an agency.

Regional Newspapers Advertising Bureau, Grosvenor House, 141 Drury Lane, London WC2B 5TD; 01-836 8251. Provides a single point of entry to advertising in any of the 1000 local newspapers.

British Rate and Data (BRAD), Maclean Hunter House, Chalk Lane, Barnet, Hertfordshire EN4 0BU; 01-441 6644. BRAD lists and describes all the UK's specialist magazines and journals that carry advertising, from *Accountancy Age* to *Wine & Spirit Monthly*. It also gives details of poster advertising, local radio, cinema and transport advertising.

British List Brokers Association, 30 Eastbourne Terrace, London W2 6LG; 01-724 0560.

Astro Mailing; 021-779 6771. Will locate any mailing list to suit your customer specification – however, to get the best you must use them for the mailing.

Publications for PR
Benn's Media Directory
Benn Publications Ltd, Sovereign Way, Tonbridge, Kent TN9 1RW

British Rate and Data
76 Oxford Street, London W1N 0HH

Hollis Press & Public Relations Annual
Contact House, Lower Hampton Road, Sudbury-on-Thames, Surrey

PRADS Media List
Press Information and Mailing Services, Faber Court, 4 St John's Place, London EC1

How will the results be checked?

A glance at the advertising analysis below will show how one organisation tackled the problem.

The table below shows the advertising results for a small business course run in London. At first glance the Sunday paper produced the most enquiries. Although it cost the most, £340, the cost per enquiry was only slightly more than the other media used. But the objective of this advertising was not simply to create interest; it was intended to sell places on the course. In fact, only 10 of the 75 enquiries were converted into orders – an advertising cost of £34 per head. On this basis the Sunday paper was between 2.5 and 3.5 times more expensive than any other medium.

Measuring advertising effect

Media used	Enquiries	Cost of advertising	Cost per enquiry	Number of customers	Advertising cost per customer
		£	£		£
Sunday paper	75	340	4.50	10	34
Daily paper	55	234	4.25	17	14
Posters	30	125	4.20	10	12
Local weekly paper	10	40	4.00	4	10
Personal recommendation	20	?	?	19	?
Total	190	739	4.35	60	18

Judy Lever, co-founder of Blooming Marvellous, the upmarket maternity-wear company, believes strongly not only in evaluating the results of advertising, but in monitoring a particular media capacity to reach her customers:

'We start off with one-sixteenth of a page ads in the specialist press,' says Judy, 'then once the medium has proved itself we progress gradually to half a page, which experience shows to be our optimum size. On average there are 700,000 pregnancies a year, but the circulation of specialist magazines is only around the 300,000 mark. We have yet to discover a way of reaching all our potential customers at the right time – in other words, early on in their pregnancies.'

The Bigmack Health Food Co (BHFC)

Advertising

BHFC will do only limited advertising in a few selected media. The amount of £750 has been allocated to print up handbills announcing the shop's 'grand' opening. These handbills will be distributed in the immediate catchment area around the shop during its first week of opening.

The amount of £75 a month has also been allocated for local advertising. Other media will be considered from time to time.

Promotion

BHFC is putting together a 'Health Food Weekend' programme that will consist of a weekend hike in the West Country. The outing will include health food meals, nightly entertainment, and leisurely hikes during the day. The event will be open to the public and will be free. This outing is scheduled for 8–10 June and BHFC has allocated £1200 for it.

BHFC is considering other promotional techniques, including a radio series of short messages on health foods, a speaker's bureau for groups interested in learning about health foods, and a newsletter to be distributed to customers, suppliers and others.

Worksheet for Assignment 8: Advertising and promotion

1. Prepare a leaflet describing your product/service to your main customers.
2. Write a press release announcing the arrival of your business on to the market. List the media to whom you will send the release.
3. Prepare an advertising and promotional plan for the upcoming year, explaining:

   (a) What you want to happen as a result of your advertising.
   (b) How much it's worth to you to make that happen.
   (c) What message(s) you will use to achieve these results.
   (d) What media you will use and why.
   (e) How the results of your advertising will be monitored.
   (f) How much you will spend.

4. If you have already done some advertising or promotional work, describe what you have done and the results you have achieved. Has your work on this assignment given you any pointers for future action?

Suggested further reading
Effective Advertising, H C Carter, Kogan Page, 1986.
The Principles of Public Relations, Harold Oxley, Kogan Page, 1987.
A Handbook of Advertising Techniques, Tony Harrison, Kogan Page, 1987.
How to Promote Your Own Business, Jim Dudley, Kogan Page, 1987.

Assignment 9
Place and Distribution

'Place' is the fourth 'P' in the marketing mix. In this aspect of your business plan you should describe exactly how you will get your products to your customers.

If you are a retailer, restaurateur or garage proprietor, for example, then your customers will come to you. Here, your physical location will most probably be the key to success. For businesses in the manufacturing field it is more likely that you will go out to 'find' customers. In this case it will be your channels of distribution that are the vital link.

Even if you are already in business and plan to stay in the same location, it would do no harm to take this opportunity to review that decision. If you are looking for additional funds to expand your business, your location will undoubtedly be an area prospective financiers will want to explore.

Location

From your market research data you should be able to come up with a list of criteria that are important to your choice of location. Here are some of the factors you need to weigh up when deciding where to locate:

1. Is there a market for the particular type of business you plan? If you're selling a product or service aimed at a particular age or socio-economic group, analyse the demographic characteristics of the area. Are there sufficient numbers of people in the relevant age and income groups? Are the numbers declining or increasing?
2. If you need skilled or specialist labour, is it readily available?
3. Are the necessary back-up services available?
4. How readily available are raw materials, components and other supplies?
5. How does the cost of premises, rates and utilities compare with other areas?
6. How accessible is the site by road, rail, air?
7. Are there any changes in the pipeline which might adversely affect trade, eg, a new motorway bypassing the town, changes in transport services, closure of a large factory?

8. Are there competing businesses in the immediate neighbourhood? Will these have a beneficial or detrimental effect?

9. Is the location conducive to the creation of a favourable market image? For instance, a high fashion designer may lack credibility trading from an area famous for its heavy industry but infamous for its dirt and pollution.

10. Is the area generally regarded as low or high growth? Is the area pro-business?

11. Can you and your key employees get to the area easily and quickly?

You may even have spotted a 'role model'; a successful competitor, perhaps in another town, who appears to have got his location spot on.

Using these criteria you can quickly screen out most unsuitable areas. Other locations may have to be visited several times, at different hours of the day and week, before screening them out.

Chantal Coady, founder of Rococo, stated in her business plan:

'Location is crucial to the success or failure of my business, therefore I have chosen the World's End section of the King's Road, Chelsea, at the junction of Beaufort Street. This is conveniently located for the Chelsea/Knightsbridge clientele. There is a good passing trade, and a generally creative ambience on this road, and no other specialist chocolate shop in the vicinity.'

World's End was not chosen on a whim, it was the subject of a most careful study. While Chantal was confident that her 'Rococo' concept was unique, she was enough of a realist to recognise that at one level it could be seen as just another upmarket chocolate shop. As such her shop needed its own distinctive catchment area. She drew up a map of chocolate shops situated in Central London which verified her closest competitors to be in Knightsbridge – in Central London terms, another world.

A further subject of concern was the nature of the passing trade in the vicinity of the proposed World's End shop. The local residents could be polled by direct leafleting, but she decided to find out more about the passing trade by means of a questionnaire. About half the people questioned responded favourably to the 'Rococo' concept.

When writing up this element of your business plan keep these points in mind:

1. Almost every benefit has a cost associated with it. This is particularly true of location. Make sure that you carefully evaluate the cost of each prospective location against the expected benefits. A saving of a couple of hundred pounds a month in rent may result in thousands of pounds of lost sales. On the other hand, don't choose a high rent

location unless you are convinced that it will result in higher profits. Higher costs do not necessarily mean greater benefits.

2. Choose the location with the business in mind. Don't start with the location as a 'given'. You may think it makes sense to put a bookshop in an unused portion of a friend's music shop since the marginal cost of the space is zero. The problem with this approach is that you force the business into a location that may or may not be adequate. If the business is 'given' (ie already decided upon) then the location should not also be given. You should choose the best location (ie the one that yields the most profit) for the business. 'Free' locations can end up being very expensive if the business is not an appropriate one.

   On the other hand, if you have a 'given' location, you should try to find the right business for the location. The business should not also be predetermined. What business provides the highest and best use of the location?

3. When you write your business plan as a financing tool, you often may not have the specific business location selected prior to completion of the business plan. This is fine, since there is no point in wasting time deciding on a location until you know you will have the money to start the business. Besides, even if you do select a location before obtaining the money, it is very possible that the location will already be gone by the time you get through the loan application process and have the business firm enough to sign a lease or purchase agreement. Another consideration is that you may wear out your welcome with an estate agent if you make a habit of withdrawing from deals at the last minute, due to lack of funds.

   It will suffice if you are able to explain exactly what type of location you will be acquiring. Knowing this, you will be able to make a good attempt at cost and sales estimates, even though the specific location has yet to be determined.

Premises

In your business plan you will need to address these issues with respect to premises:

1. Can the premises you want be used for your intended business? The main categories of 'use' are retail, office, light industrial, general industrial and special categories. If your business falls into a different category from that of a previous occupant you may have to apply to the local authority for a 'change of use'.

   An unhappy illustration of this came from a West Country builder who bought a food shop with living accommodation above. His intention was to sell paint and decorative products below and house his family above. Within three months of launching his venture he was advised that as his shop stock was highly flammable, the house would need fire retardant floors, ceilings and doors – at a cost of £20,000, even doing the work himself. The business was effectively killed off before it started.

2. Will you be making any structural alterations? If so, planning permission may be needed and building regulations must be complied with. Both take time and should be allowed for in your cash flow projections.

3. Are the premises the appropriate size? It is always difficult to calculate just how much space you'll require, since your initial preoccupation is probably just surviving. Generally, you won't want to use valuable cash to acquire unnecessarily large premises. However, if you make it past the starting post you will inevitably grow, and if you haven't room to expand you'll have to begin looking for premises all over again. This can be expensive, not to say disruptive.

Equinox, whose founder attended a Cranfield enterprise programme, got over this problem by renting a Beehive unit from English Industrial Estates. These units are ready to use with all services connected and available on quarterly agreements. Equinox started in a 500 sq ft unit, expanded into next door to make 1000 sq ft of space, and at the start of their third year moved over the road into 3000 sq ft. Removal costs and disruption were thus kept to a minimum.

One other possible solution is to take larger premises than you initially require and sublet the surplus accommodation on a short-term lease (provided the landlord agrees). If this isn't possible, it's more prudent to think small and gauge your requirements by where your business plan suggests you'll be in two or three years time.

To calculate your space requirements, prepare a layout which indicates the ideal position for the equipment you will need, allowing adequate circulation space. Shops require counters, display stands, refrigeration units etc. In a factory, machinery may not only need careful positioning but you may have to consider in great detail the safe positioning of electricity cables, waste pipes, air extractors etc.

Make cut-out scale models of the various items and lay these on scaled drawings of different size premises – 400 sq ft, 1000 sq ft etc.

By a process of trial and error you should arrive at an arrangement which is flexible, easy to operate, pleasant to look at, accessible for maintenance, and comfortable for both staff and customers. Only now can you calculate the likely cost of premises to include in your business plan.

4. Will the premises conform with existing fire, health and safety regulations? The Health & Safety at Work Act (1974), the Factories Act (1961), The Offices, Shops & Railway Premises Act (1963) and the Fire Precautions Act (1971) set out the conditions under which most workers, including the self-employed and members of the public at large, can be present. (The Health & Safety Commission, Regina House, 259 Marylebone Road, London NW1 5RR; 01-723 1262, can advise.)

5. If you plan to work from home, have you checked that you are not prohibited from doing so by the house deeds, or whether your type of activity is likely to irritate the neighbours? This route into business is much in favour with sources of debt finance as it is seen to lower the risks during the vulnerable start-up period. Venture capitalists, on the other hand, would probably see it as a sign of 'thinking too small' and steer clear of the proposition. Nevertheless, working from home can make sound sense.

> For example, Peter Robertson, aged 20, who founded Road Runner Despatch in November 1983, started out running his business as a very domestic affair. Operated from his home in Brightlingsea, Essex, his mother answered the telephone and frequently his father used the family car to make collections. Within two years he was employing 10 full-time motorcycle riders. Only at this stage did Robertson put together a plan, which involved raising £100,000 capital, to open an office on a central site, complete with a state-of-the-art radio telephone system.

6. Will you lease or buy? Purchasing premises outright frequently makes sense for an established, viable business as a means of increasing its asset base. But for a start-up, interest and repayments on the borrowings will usually be more than the rental payments. Some financiers feel that your business idea should be capable of making more profit than the return you could expect from property. On this basis you should put the capital to be raised into 'useful' assets such as plant, equipment, stocks etc.

However, some believe that if you intend to spend any money on converting or improving the premises, doing so to leased property is simply improving the landlord's investment and wasting your (their) money.

In any event your backers will want to see a lease long enough to see your business firmly established and secure enough to allow you to stay on if it is essential to the survival of your business. Starting up a restaurant in short-lease premises, for example, would be a poor investment proposition.

7. If appropriate, you could consider locating in a sympathetic and supportive environment. For example, universities and colleges often have a Science Park on campus, with premises and starter units for high-tech ventures. Enterprise agencies often have offices, workshops and small industrial units attached. In these situations you may have access to a telex, fax, computer, accounting service and business advice, on a pay-as-you-use basis. This would probably be viewed as a plus point by any prospective financial backer.

8. What opening/works hours do you plan to keep, and why?

Channels of distribution

If your customers don't come to you then you have the following options in getting your product or service to them. Your business plan should explain which you have chosen and why.

- *Retail stores.* This general name covers the great range of outlets from the corner shop to Harrods. Some offer speciality goods such as hi-fi equipment, where the customer expects professional help from the staff. Others, such as Marks & Spencer and Tesco, are mostly self-service, with customers making up their own minds on choice of product.
- *Wholesalers.* The pattern of wholesale distribution has changed out of all recognition over the past two decades. It is still an extremely important channel where physical distribution, stock holding, finance and breaking bulk are still profitable functions.
- *Cash and carry.* This slightly confusing route has replaced the traditional wholesaler as a source of supply for smaller retailers. In return for paying cash and picking up the goods yourself, the 'wholesaler' shares part of his profit margin with you. The attraction for the wholesaler is improved cash flow and for the retailer a bigger margin and a wide product range. Hypermarkets and discount stores also fit somewhere between the manufacturer and the market-place.
- *Mail order.* This specialised technique provides a direct channel to the customer, and is an increasingly popular route for new small businesses.

> Peter Howcroft, who built his 'casuals with toughness and durability' business, Rohan, from modest beginnings in the early 1980s, when he had just £60 in the bank, to a £7 million business in 1987, puts much of his success down to changing distribution channels. Until 1982 most of his sales were to retail shops, who either wouldn't take

enough produce or didn't pay up when they did. That summer he set up his mail order branch, using his box of enquiries and letters built up over the years as a mailing list. He moved a year's sales in two months, getting all the cash in up front.

Other direct from 'producer to customer' channels include:

- *Door-to-door selling*. Traditionally used by vacuum cleaner distributors and encyclopaedia companies, this is now used by insurance companies, cavity wall insulation firms, double glazing firms and others. Many use hard-sell techniques, giving door-to-door selling a bad name. However, Avon Cosmetics have managed to sell successfully door-to-door without attracting the stigma of unethical selling practices.
- *Party plan selling*. A variation on door-to-door selling which is on the increase with new party plan ideas arriving from the USA. Agents enrolled by the company invite their friends to a get-together where the products are demonstrated and orders are invited. The agent gets a commission. Party plan has worked very well for Tupperware and other firms who sell this way.

  On a more modest scale, one man turned his hobby of making pine bookcases and spice racks into a profitable business by getting his wife to invite neighbours for coffee mornings where his wares were prominently displayed.
- *Telephone selling*. This too can be a way of moving goods in one single step, from 'maker' to consumer. Few products can be sold easily in this way; however, repeat business is often secured via the phone.

Selecting distribution channels

These are the factors you should consider when choosing channels of distribution for your particular business:

1. *Does it meet your customers' needs?* You have to find out how your customers expect their product or service to be delivered to them and why they need that particular route.
2. *Will the product itself survive?* Fresh vegetables, for example, need to be moved quickly from where they are grown to where they are consumed.
3. *Can you sell enough this way?* 'Enough' is how much you *want* to sell. Sinclair launched his microvision TV by direct mail because he wanted to *restrict* demand to match his limited capacity to supply.
4. *Is it compatible with your image?* If you are selling a luxury product,

then door-to-door selling may spoil the impression you are trying to create in the rest of your marketing effort.

5. *How do your competitors distribute?* If they have been around for a while and are obviously successful it is well worth looking at how your competitors distribute and using that knowledge to your advantage.

6. *Will the channel be cost effective?* A small manufacturer may not find it cost effective to sell to retailers west of Bristol because the direct 'drop' size, that is the load per order, is too small to be worthwhile.

7. *Will the mark-up be enough?* If your product cannot bear at least a 100 per cent mark-up, then it is unlikely that you will be able to sell it through department stores. Your distribution channel has to be able to make a profit from selling your product too.

8. *Push-pull.* Moving a product through a distribution channel calls for two sorts of selling activity. *Push* is the name given to selling your product in, for example, a shop. *Pull* is the effort that you carry out on the shop's behalf to help them to sell your product out of that shop. That pull may be caused by your national advertising, a merchandising activity, or the uniqueness of your product. You need to know how much push and pull are needed for the channel you are considering. If you are not geared up to help retailers to sell out your product, and they need that help, then this could be a poor channel.

Historical Connections, a new company established in 1988 to market educational wall charts, faced conflicting distribution issues. Its produce had to be securely and economically packed in such a way that the charts could be unrolled, crease free, by the end user; at the same time the product had to occupy an acceptable amount of shelf space in a crowded gift shop, for example.

A cardboard tube was the obvious answer to these problems; however, that rendered the true 'value' of the product invisible to shoppers. This problem was in turn overcome by providing retailers with a framed chart, positioned by Historical Connections' sales people, when the account was opened.

This simple 'point of sale' display was an elegant and cost effective 'pull'.

---

9. *Physical distribution.* The way in which you have to move your product to your end customer is also an important factor to weigh up when choosing a channel. As well as such factors as the cost of carriage, you will also have to decide about packaging materials. As a rough rule of thumb, the more stages in the distribution channel the more robust and expensive your packaging will have to be.

10. *Cash flow.* Not all channels of distribution settle their bills promptly.

Mail order customers, for example, will pay in advance, but retailers can take up to 90 days or more. You need to take account of this settlement period in your cash flow forecast.

Worksheet for Assignment 9: Place and distribution

1. What type and size of premises is required for your business?
2. Describe the location.
3. Why do you need this type of premises and location? What competitive advantage does it give you?
4. If freehold:
   Value   _____
   Mortgage outstanding   _____
   Monthly repayments   _____
   Mortgage with whom   _____
5. If leasehold:
   Unexpired period of lease   _____
   Is there an option to renew?   _____
   Present rent payment   _____
   Date of rent payment   _____
   Date of next rent review   _____

6. What rates are payable on your business premises?
7. What are the insurance details?
   Amount   _____
   Premium   _____

8. Are these premises adequate for your future needs? If not, what plans do you have?
9. If you have not found your premises yet, what plans do you have to find them?
10. What channels of distribution are used in your field; which do you plan to use and why?

Suggested further reading

Effective Marketing Management, Ch 6, 'Getting the Place Right', Martin Christopher and Malcolm MacDonald, Open University, 1986.

How to Choose Business Premises, H Green, B Chalkley, P Foley, Kogan Page, 1986.

Running Your Own Mail Order Business, Malcolm Breckman, Kogan Page, 1987.

Phase 4
Operations

Assignment 10
The Operations Plan

Operations is the general name given to all the activities required to implement strategy. So, for example, once you have decided what to sell, to whom and at what price, you may still need to find someone to make your product, sell it, and deliver it. You may also need to take out insurance, draw up contracts of employment, print stationery, and recruit staff, for example.

Of necessity, the emphasis you put on each element of this assignment will depend entirely on the nature of your business.

Your business plan need not show the complete detail as to how every operational activity will be implemented. Clearly, you and your colleagues will need to know, but for the business plan it is sufficient to show that you have taken account of the principal matters that concern your venture, and have a workable solution in hand.

The following are some of the most important operational issues to be addressed in your business plan.

Selling and sales management

Anyone considering backing your business will look long and hard at how you plan to sell. Unbelievably, it is an area often dismissed in a couple of lines in a business plan. That error alone is enough to turn off most investors. Your business plan should provide answers to these questions:

- Who will conduct the selling for your business, and have they been professionally trained to sell?

   Howard Fabian's business was designing and selling greetings cards. His main market was London and the south-east, where there were 120 important shops to be sold to. He planned to sell to these accounts himself. This meant visiting all the outlets once at the outset. He could make four to five calls a day, so it would take between four and five weeks to cover the ground. After that he would visit the most important 30 every month, the next 30 every two months, and he would phone or visit the remainder from time to time, and send samples of new designs in the hope of encouraging them to order. While on an enterprise programme at Cranfield he took a professional selling skills course.

Outside London and the south-east, Howard proposed to appoint agents, based in the principal provincial cities. To recruit these he planned to use trade press and the Manufacturers Agents Register. Each appointment would be made on a three-month trial basis, and he had an agency contract explaining this business relationship drawn up. He proposed to set each agent a performance target based on the population in this catchment area. Sales within 25 per cent of target would be acceptable; outside that figure he would review the agent's contract.

Initially he was looking for 10 agents, who he would visit and go out with once a quarter.

As selling time in a shop was short, it was important that he and his agents should have a minimum set agenda of points to cover, and a sales presenter to show the range quickly and easily from the standing position.

- What selling methods will you employ? For example, telephone selling, cold calling, following up leads from mail shots and advertising etc.

In Graham Davy's Equinox designer furniture business, his principal potential customers were furniture retailers. This was too large and widespread a target audience to sell to without some specific focus.

First, he boxed in an area bounded by Bristol, London and St Albans – effectively the wedge between the M4 and M40 motorways. He felt this was a large enough area of affluent users to support his modest production capacity. From desk research he identified the names and addresses of 250 prospective customers. He mailed his brochure to every one of these and then called on the 40 or so most likely firms. In the meantime his partner telephoned the remaining firms to gauge reaction and see if they were 'worth' visiting.

In the first six months they got five customers, two of whom had given repeat business and were prepared to place orders by phone.

The next year they attended an exhibition which resulted in 25 potential customers completing enquiry slips on their stand. These were followed up and a further six customers were secured. By the third year, Equinox had 23 customers, all of whom had placed repeat business.

- If you plan to sell to retailers, what point-of-sale material will you use to attract purchasers?
- Who will direct, monitor and control your sales effort and what experience/skills do they have?

144

- What sales volume and activity targets, such as calls per day etc, have you set for each sales person or selling method?
- What selling aids such as leaflets, brochures, videos, technical back-up etc, will you provide? Include also any details on in-house sales support, such as technical service, telesales etc.
- How do you plan to impart full 'product' knowledge to your sales team?

Paul Howcroft, who has taken his Rohan clothing company from a standing start less than a decade ago to a £7 million business in 1987, puts much of that success down to the fact that all his staff are trained so that they can talk sensibly about the products with any of their 300,000 customers.

- What objections do you anticipate from prospective customers, and what arguments do you have to meet these?
- Who exactly makes the buying decision, and which other people can influence that decision?
- How long is the process from becoming aware of your product or service, to making the buying decision, receiving the product or service and finally paying for it?

This will have an important bearing on your cash flow and initial sales forecast, as the examples that follow will illustrate.

Medsoft was set up to sell dedicated micro-computer systems to hospital consultants. The business concept grew out of a chance meeting at a computer exhibition between Richard Kensall, then a successful department store owner and slightly disillusioned computer dealer, and an up-and-coming young doctor with a love of computers.

The doctor's problem was that he had too large a volume of patient data to classify and analyse. Some 16,000 consultants had a need to record details on 35 million patient attendances and 5 million in-patients per annum. For each patient a record had to be generated containing all details concerning the patient, their clinical history and indications, clinical tests, results, diagnoses, operations, complications and follow-up care. In 1980, almost all such patient records were generated and maintained manually.

So, for Medsoft the market opportunity was substantial and with some further development their product range was proven. The only problem was the time taken to get a decision made as to whether to buy or not, and then to get the cash in.

Capital investment decisions such as this follow a long and complex procedure in the UK hospital service. From finding a consultant who wanted to buy, to encouraging him to write out a project proposal, getting that proposal through the hospital committee, on to endorsement from the district management team and then finally to approval by the Regional Scientific Officer, could take up to nine months. Even when over all these hurdles a project could fail if the region had insufficient funds to pay for all the properly approved proposals. To add insult to injury, under these circumstances all proposals start again at the bottom of the pile.

With this process in mind, Medsoft's business plan had to anticipate zero sales revenue for the first nine months at least, and only modest sums thereafter until well into the second year. Their resultant cash flow forecast looked very sick indeed over this period, but in their business plan they were able to provide a satisfactory argument for this situation occurring.

Medsoft decision-making process

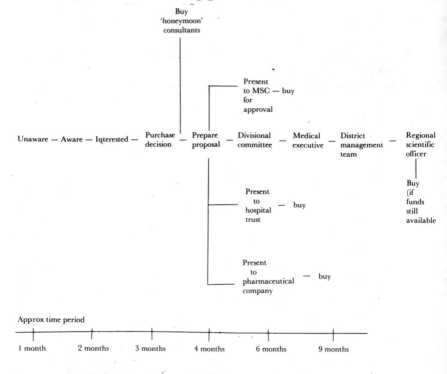

Fortunately, while investigating the decision-making process they uncovered four types of potential customer who could 'buy' within six months. Newly appointed hospital consultants were unofficially awarded £30,000 for capital expenditure on appointment; some hospitals had their own trust funds; some consultants had close ties with pharmaceutical companies who would support their 'pet' pro-

146

jects; and some consultants had experience of getting government grants from such organisations as the Manpower Services Commission. These people were to be the focus of all sales effort for the first six months of Medsoft's life.

- What incentives are there for people to meet targets and how will you motivate them to do so?
- What value of orders are currently on hand, or are expected in the immediate future, and from whom?
- What procedures do you have for handling customer complaints?

Manufacturing

If your business involves making or constructing products then you should address the following issues in the business plan:

- Will you make the product yourself, or buy in either ready to sell, or as components for assembly? One Cranfield graduate enterprise programme had these examples of different types of operation:

> Jenny Row designed her knitwear herself, but had it made up by outworkers. In this way she could expand or contract output quickly, paying only the extra cost of materials and production, for more orders. It also left her free to design new toys to add to her existing range.

> Tim Brown sold computer systems tailormade to carry out solicitors' conveyancing work. He commissioned software writers to prepare the programs, bought in computers from the manufacturer and selected a range of printers to suit individual customers' requirements. His end product was a total system, which he bought in 'kit' parts from his various sub-contractors. Apart from IBM and a handful of giants no one company could produce all these elements in-house.

> Graham Davy designed and manufactured his own range of furniture. He rented a Beehive workshop and bought in cutting, turning and polishing tools, and a finish spraying room. He bought in wood, worked on it himself, producing batches of three or four of each design. The equipment needed for design and prototype work was also sufficient for small batch production.

You should also explain why you have chosen your manufacturing route.
- Describe the manufacturing process to be used, and if appropriate explain how your principal competitors go about their manufacturing.

Jon Newall's company, Escargot Anglais Ltd, was set up in 1987 to make and market snails in the UK. The production system he adopted had already been used with some considerable success at one of the world's largest snail ranches in California. The stages of production are as follows:

Commencing production. Breeding snails will be fed on a compound with the essential requirements of a low copper content (below 13–14 mg/kg) and no anticoccidiostat, but with an appropriate calcium content for good shell disposition.

Growing young snails. These are grown in 25-litre buckets in batches of 150.

Fattening and finishing. At three months the snails will have attained market weight. They are then processed and frozen on site. For this boiling and freezing equipment is needed, costing around £2500 per line packaging. Finally, snails will be packaged in batches of six in a moulded aluminium foil dish, covered in shrinkwrap, with promotional material on the front, and recipes on the back. Equipment for packaging will cost around £2000.

- What plant and equipment will you need and what output limits will they have (see table below)?
- Provide a rough sketch of the layout of your manufacturing unit, showing the overall size of facility needed, the positioning of equipment etc, and the path of materials and finished goods.
- What engineering support, if any, will you need?
- How will you monitor and control quality?

Plant equipment	Process (what does it do?)	Maximum volume	Cost	Do you already own it?
Total cost of equipment to be acquired			£	

Materials and sources of supply

Your business plan should also explain what bought-in materials you require, who you will buy them from, and how much they will cost.

Returning to Escargot Anglais Ltd, Jon Newall explained in his business plan how he chose his main source of supply:

'The breeding snails were at first fed on vegetable waste obtained free in abundance from local greengrocers. While at first this seemed a very attractive proposition which I have seen work well in France and elsewhere, local supplies were unsatisfactory. The high water content led to difficulties in disposing of waste matter but, most importantly, residual pesticides, particularly in the more succulent leafy matter, led to a high snail fatality rate.

After much experimenting I found a chicken feed, 'Pauls Traditional 18', which has all the essential ingredients. It can be bought from the local wholesaler for £4.60 per 25kg bag. My original budgets were based on the assumption that free vegetable waste would be used; this is no longer valid and all feeding stuffs will have to be bought in. This will increase costs by about £7000 per annum and so reduce gross profits. However, apart from capital expenditure on boiling, freezing and packaging equipment (total £4500) the only non-labour cost apart from feeding stuffs is for packaging materials, butter and garlic. These will be bought in, locally at first; however, I am looking at the possibility of purchasing cheap EEC butter surplus.'

- What major items of bought-in materials or services will you require?
- Who could supply those and what are the terms and conditions of sale?
- Why have you chosen your supplier(s)?

People

People are the most important element of any business venture. However good or innovative the business idea, or competitive the strategy, absolutely nothing can get done without people.

For F International, the £10 million consultancy business with offices in Chesham and Berkhamsted, people are the business. The cost flexibility that comes from having a workforce that consists primarily of part-time freelance staff – working mothers – provides F International's key competitive advantage. It can respond to market changes without having to hire or fire large numbers.

The company's backbone consists of a pool of 817 freelance (hence the F) computer programmers, supplemented by a core of 120 full-time and 140 part-time managerial and administrative staff. This high ratio of management to staff workers underlines the degree of organisation required to run such a decentralised group, who for the most part work from home.

'The office is no more than a bit of glue that holds us together', says Steve Shirley, who founded F International when she was 28 years old.

Your business plan should explain which people are important to your venture and should provide answers to the following questions.

- Have you written job descriptions for each key position in your business? A summary of responsibilities should appear in your business plan.

    Michael Golder, who grew the £65 million a year Kennedy Brooks business from a single restaurant in just seven years, gives each of his 4000 employees a 'staff handbook'. This contains every detail of their duties, right down to having clean fingernails.

- The Employment Protection (Consolidations) Act 1978 requires you to issue every employee who works more than 16 hours per week with a written statement of the main terms and conditions of their employment within 13 weeks of starting work. Have you made arrangements for this?
- Are all key positions filled? If not, how do you plan to recruit and select these people?

    Carolyn Lowing made this entry in her business plan to raise £120,000 for the Oriental, a Cambridge based martial arts centre:

    Initially I shall be responsible for setting up the enterprise. Before opening the centre a part-time assistant will be taken on to help with administration and the day-to-day matters, leaving me free to concentrate on promoting the centre and attracting clients, as well as organising the first few courses and the opening event. Further part-time assistants will be employed when the workload gets such that individual posts can be justified. This stage should be reached about three months after opening.

    The first assistant will be responsible for secretarial and administrative duties as well as acting as receptionist and bar staff. These responsibilities will later be mainly administration and office duties as extra staff are taken on as reception and bar staff and for general duties.

    An outside contractor may be employed for the cleaning of the centre following this expansion in staff requirements.

    The local Cambridge paper will be a suitable place to advertise for all these appointments. I have two people in mind for my first part-time assistant, both of whom have wide, relevant experience and are available now.

- What wage and salary levels have you set for employees? How do these compare with other similar employers in the area?
- What arrangements have you made to handle Pay As You Earn, National Insurance, and pensions?
- Health and safety at work are a legal responsibility of employers. Are you aware of the terms and conditions of the various Acts of Parliament, and their likely cost implication for your business?
- Training, from induction to job training, are also factors to be considered at the outset, and their costs allowed for in your business plan. You may be eligible for subsidised instruction from one of the various government agencies responsible for this.

> Debra Turkington, a Californian who established her business 'California Cake & Cookie Company' in Govan, Scotland in 1985, incorporated her ideas on training into her business plan. With her belief in the value of 'investing in people', Debra recognised from the outset that as the business grew she needed to train her managers if she was to make the business run profitably:
>
> 'Never underestimate the ability and potential of your staff. If I could understand what a balance sheet meant there was no reason why they shouldn't and as a result of the training they had a much better grasp of what made the company work. That meant they could help the company to move forward more effectively.'
>
> Since Debra started running her training programme for her young managers she has seen her gross margin increase by 5 per cent and productivity rise substantially. What's more, the quality of the product has risen as well, with the result that her company is among the fastest growing in the West of Scotland.

- What back-up do you have if you or any other key person is ill, or absent for any reason?

> The reasons for absence can be quite obscure, as one new business founder recently discovered. He became one of the 400,000 or so people in the UK who annually receive a summons to do compulsory but unpaid jury service. The libel trial he was called to attend lasted approximately three weeks, which he remarked set him back nearly six months! He could have insured against such an event and received sufficient funds either to buy in help or compensate for loss of profits.

- Do you expect your employees to dress in a particular style for work, or to wear uniform?

Legal and insurance issues

Every venture will have to address some legal and insurance issues. Certain insurance, such as Employers and Public Liability cover, is compulsory for all businesses and there are certain forms of insurance which are compulsory in law for specific businesses. Other forms of insurance are voluntary.

As far as your business plan is concerned, these issues will always be raised by potential backers:

● What will your terms and conditions of sale be and are they printed on your order acceptance stationery?

> One unfortunate entrepreneur felt that his business, a management training consultancy, had got off to a good start when his first client, a major American computer company, booked him for three courses. Just three weeks prior to the first of these courses, and after he had carried out all the preparatory work, prepared relevant examples, handouts etc, the client cancelled the order. The reason given was a change in 'policy' on training dictated by their overseas parent company.
>
> If this entrepreneur had included in his standard terms and conditions a cancellation clause, then he would have received adequate compensation. In fact, he was operating on a 'wing and a prayer', had no terms of trade, and wasn't even aware there was an industrial 'norm'. Most of his competitors charged 100 per cent cancellation fee for cancellations within three weeks, 50 per cent within six weeks, 25 per cent within eight weeks, and thereafter no charge.

● Are your premises, equipment and stocks adequately insured? By way of illustrating the need to take professional advice in these matters, the following incident was related to the enterprise programme class at Cranfield:

> A newly established business, planning to expand its activities economically, sought and found a specialist supplier of second hand reconditioned woodworking machinery – lathes, turners, band saws etc. After inspecting the machinery in Yorkshire, they arranged for it to be transported by the vendor under his own goods in transit insurance cover to their factory in the West Country.
>
> While a particularly heavy piece was being unloaded, it fell from the transporter on to the ground immediately outside their factory, and was damaged beyond repair. Their own insurance only covered machinery inside their workshop, the vendor's only while the goods were on the transporter. The gap in between was an insurance 'no man's land', where neither party had cover. As a result the entrepre-

neur lost £3000 but learnt a lot about the value of taking professional advice.

- Have you arranged for employers' liability cover and public liability and product liability?
- If you are offering expert advice, are you protected against claims for negligence from your clients?
- If your business is one of the hundred or so which require licensing before they can operate, what steps have you taken to obtain a licence?

Worksheet for Assignment 10: The operations plan

Describe briefly the main operational aspects that are involved in ensuring that your strategy is successfully implemented. In particular, you should consider:

1. Who will sell for you?
2. What selling methods will they employ?
3. Will you use point of sale material, leaflets, brochures or videos, for example?
4. Who will manage, monitor and control your sales effort and how will they do so?
5. Describe the selling process leading from an unaware prospect to a converted client, covering identification of decision makers, overcoming objections, gaining agreement etc.
6. Will you make your product yourself or buy it in – and why?
7. If you are making a product, describe the production process; also explain how your principal competitors go about manufacturing.
8. What plant and equipment will you need, what can it do, how much will it cost and where will you get it from?
9. What bought-in materials and/or services will you need, where will you buy them from and how much will they cost?
10. What employees will you need in your business? If they are not already recruited, how will you go about finding them?
11. What arrangements have you made for contracts of employment, job descriptions, wages and salary levels, training, payroll processing etc?
12. What back-up do you have if you or any other key staff are absent?
13. Have you examined any likely legal issues that might affect your venture, such as conditions of sale?
14. Have you examined any likely insurance issues that might affect your venture, such as employers, public or product liability cover, or premises, equipment and stock insurance?

Suggested further reading

Selling by Telephone, Len Rogers, Kogan Page, 1986.
Managing a Sales Team, Neil R Sweeney, Kogan Page, 1983.
Winning Strategies for Managing People, Robert Irwin and Rota Wolenik, Kogan Page, 1986.
Getting Sales, R D Smith and G Dick, Kogan Page, 1984.
Profit Sharing and Profitability, Bell & Hanson, Kogan Page, 1987.
Law for the Small Business, 6th edition, Pat Clayton, Kogan Page, 1988.
Small Beginnings (Small Scale Manufacturing Methods), Alan Bollard, Intermediate Technology Publications, 1983.

Phase 5
Forecasting Results

Introduction

Once you have formulated a basic or new strategy for your business, you will have to make some forecast of the likely results of your endeavours. These projections are essential to show how much cash you will need, how much profit you could make, and to chart a safe financial strategy. This is the part of your business plan of greatest interest to potential investors and lenders.

Assignment 11
The Sales Forecast

The sales forecast is perhaps the most important set of numbers to come out of the business planning process so far. These sales figures are used to predict the cash flow forecast, the pro forma profit and loss account, and ultimately the viability of the whole venture.

These projections are also the key to valuing the business, and so they will determine whether or not bankers will lend and investors invest. Furthermore, they will give some guidance as to how much of an enterprise investors expect in exchange for funding, as some sort of price/earnings multiple rates will be used nationally to value the company.

Naturally enough, potential backers don't accept a sales forecast unchallenged, as in their experience new ventures nearly always miss the target by a wide margin.

While all forecasts may turn out to be wrong, it is important to demonstrate in your business plan that you have thought through the factors that will impact on performance. You should also show how you can deliver satisfactory results even when many of these factors work against you. Backers will be measuring the 'downside' risk, to evaluate the worst scenario and its likely effects, as well as looking towards an ultimate exit route.

Here are some guidelines to help to make an initial sales forecast. While these apply in part at least to all the financial projections an enterprise has to make, it will be more useful to take each item in turn, starting with the sales forecast. Later sections will cover the profit and loss account, cash flow, balance sheet and break-even.

- Your overall projections will have to be believable. Most lenders and investors will have an extensive experience of similar business proposals. Unlike yourself they will have the benefit of hindsight, being able to look back several years at other ventures they have backed, and see how they fared in practice as compared with their initial forecasts.

  Eurotunnel, a larger than average new business, failed to get the institutional backing it hoped for in its 1987 share flotation. While the

stock market crash had a bearing on the failure, city analysts concentrated their arguments on the 'believability' of the company's forecasts. Those forecasts were, to quote a *Times* leader, 'a little too good to be true'. Crucial passenger and freight volume forecasts were hiked up 40 per cent on the management's earlier figures and its market share projection was 12 per cent higher. They were not believable and the share offer was consequently undersubscribed.

You could gather some useful knowledge on similar businesses yourself by researching the records at Companies House, where the accounts of most companies are kept, or by talking with the founders of similar ventures, who will not be your direct competitors.

One participant on a Cranfield enterprise programme wanted to set up a single product retailing chain along the lines of the Sock Shop. Through an introduction provided from a Cranfield professor, he contacted Sophie Mirman and got the facts of what the early years could look like, from 'the horse's mouth'. Eventually, this knowledge was to carry some weight when he presented his business plan.

- How big is the market for your product or service? Is it growing or contracting? What is the economic and competitive position? These are all factors which can provide a market share basis for your forecasts. An entry market share of more than a few per cent would be most unusual. But beware of turning this argument on its head. No investor will be impressed by unsubstantiated statements such as, 'In a market of £1 billion per annum we can easily capture 1 per cent, which is £1 million a year.'
- How many customers and potential customers do you know who are likely to buy from you, and how much might they buy? Here you can use many types of data on which to base reasonable sales projections. You can interview a sample of prospective customers, issue a press release or advertisement to gauge response, and exhibit at trade shows to obtain customer reactions. If your product or service needs to be on an approved list before it can be bought, then your business plan should confirm you have that approval – or less desirably, show how you will get it.

    You should also look at seasonal factors that might cause sales to be high or low at certain periods in the year. This will be particularly significant for cash flow projections.
- For some businesses there are rules of thumb that can be used to estimate sales. This is particularly true in retailing where location studies, traffic counts and population density are known factors.

Martin Caldicott, who founded his second restaurant, Martins, in

159

London's Baker Street, with substantial backing from private City investors, used one such rule. In his experience, once a restaurant has served 30,000 clients they can expect sufficient repeat business to break even. In his first eight months of operation he had achieved 20,000.

- The 'desired income' approach embraces the concept that forecasts may also accommodate the realistic aims of the proprietor. Indeed, you could go further and state that the whole purpose of strategy is to ensure that certain forecasts are achieved. In a mature company with proven products and markets, this is more likely to be the case than with a start-up.

  Nevertheless, an element of 'How much do we need to earn?' must play a part in forecasting, if only to signal when a business idea is not worth pursuing.

  One participant on a Cranfield enterprise programme was of the opinion that if he couldn't earn at least £20,000 per annum in the second year of his new business, he wouldn't want to start up. His predicted profit margin was 20 per cent, so this 'objective' called for a sales 'forecast' of £100,000. He used his market research and the resultant strategies to satisfy himself (and his backers) that this was a realistic goal.

- One extreme of the 'desired income' approach to forecasting comes from those entrepreneurs who think that the forecasts *are* the business plan. Such people cover the business plan with a mass of largely unconnected numbers. These 'spreadsheet merchants', with reams of computer print-out covering every variation possible in business, complete with sensitivity analysis, are invariably a big turn-off with financiers.

  A senior manager in a major UK clearing bank that also has a substantial venture capital arm, has told us that he expects a set of solid, well argued financial projections, with perhaps one set of variations to illustrate that the business could survive if conditions are not quite as optimistic as calculated in the basic plan.

- As investors are aware most forecasts are usually made using rose-tinted glasses; there is certainly no room for false modesty.

  The management team of a computer software company presenting their business plan to a venture capital panel showed a sales and profit growth rate of 20 per cent annually, believing it was presenting itself as 'attractively conservative'. This led to an annual sales level of only about £500,000, with profits of £50,000 after five years. These figures were far too low to attract venture capital investment, especially in the computer software field. (Lotus Development, an extreme example in this field, went from zero to £40 million sales in two years!)

● The product life cycle can provide a useful guide to the likely pattern that sales might take over the early months and years of a new business (see below).

Product life cycle

Whenever a new business starts up, it is usually introducing a substitute for something else. If you open a new restaurant or photocopying shop, for example, it is highly unlikely you will be introducing the idea of eating out or taking copies into the neighbourhood. You will be in competition with established, albeit different businesses. For example, people may have travelled miles to find a specialist photocopy shop, or used an unsophisticated or slow machine in a local estate agent's office. Even after you set up they will continue in their old habits.

So even if your new business succeeds at the introductory phase, demand for your products or services will only grow slowly. During the growth phase things can be very different. Your product benefits become accepted – people give up travelling miles to their previous

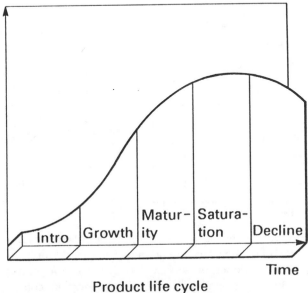

Product life cycle

161

supplier and reject the unsatisfactory machine in the local professional offices. Sales can build up very rapidly, as the three examples shown below from the micro-computer software industry demonstrate. As an interesting aside, neither Bill Gates who founded Microsoft nor Mitch Kapar, the brain behind Lotus, had programming skills when they started up and both were under 35 when they made their first million.

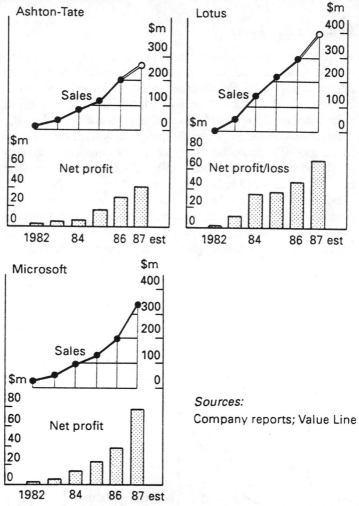

Sources:
Company reports; Value Line

However, no market is infinitely expandable. Eventually everyone has heard of the new service and most users are coming to you. At this stage your product or service has reached the maturity phase. Typically, at this phase not only will your original competitors have reacted to your entry into the market, but new ones will have been tempted in, culminating in market saturation. This phase concludes that there are too many competitors, and a usually counter-productive price war errupts. The fittest survive, but the majority of new businesses plateau at best or decline and die at worst.

The length of each phase varies from market to market:

> The founders of Dragon Lock, participants on a Cranfield enterprise programme, forecast their Rubik Cube type product would move from introduction to maturity in 18 months. The growth phase was actually reached in a few weeks.

> Another programme participant didn't anticipate reaching the growth phase for three years – and subsequent events proved even that forecast to be too optimistic.

• Finally, how far ahead should you forecast? Opinions are divided between three and five years ahead. However, financiers we have talked to, while often asking for a five-year view, only pay serious attention to the first three years.

The arguments for looking this far ahead are twofold. First, most new ventures are at their greatest risk in the first few years, so investors and lenders want to see that the proprietors have a well thought out strategy to cover this period. Second, venture capitalists in particular want to look forward to the time when they can realise their investment and move on. Typically their exit route has to materialise between years 3 and 5 – hopefully the earlier of the two.

The first two years of the sales forecast should be made on a monthly basis, and the remaining three years on a quarterly basis.

The examples below provide a flavour of the range of possible outcomes for the first few years of a new venture's life.

> Graham Brown runs Oasis, a chain of six shops, three concessions, a wholesale business and a chain of franchised outlets. He opened his first shop in Oxford in 1974, a year after completing his economics degree, and two years later his second opened in Brighton. Finding that running two shops was very different from running one, he took on a partner, Andrew Thomas, who had learnt his retailing at Debenhams and Habitat. In 1978 they raised £100,000 to open their Guildford store and in 1982 their Covent Garden flagship was opened. This cost £65,000 for shopfitting alone. By 1984 turnover was up to £3.5 million a year.

> Blooming Marvellous, a mail order company providing stylish and imaginative maternity clothes, is the brainchild of two successful career women, Judy Lever and Vivienne Pringle. Started on a shoestring with £750 and only two dresses on offer, within two and a

half years Blooming Marvellous has built up to an annual turnover of £120,000.

Brian Davies, a former sales manager, and his wife Anne bought the Rothesay, a middle-market 23-bedroomed private hotel at Llandudno, North Wales, for £55,000 in 1978. They spent the summer of that year learning the ins and outs of the hotel trade under the guidance of the previous owners. Total turnover for that year was £37,925.

In 1979 Davies introduced a new sales strategy and cold-called on tour companies to drum up new business. This succeeded in raising turnover for that year to £54,134.

1980 saw Davies making improvements to the decor and restaurant facilities, but several coach cancellations caused by the recession left total revenue for the year at £60,816.

In 1981 they consolidated past strategies and turnover rose to £64,844 but, with some costing savings, profits grew faster than turnover.

The strategy for 1982 was to extend the season from its previous 17 weeks into the 20–22 range. Unfortunately, unusually bad weather reduced the casual trade by 12 per cent, but coach party sales were a record. The resultant sales level peaked at £73,950.

Maureen and Graham Davy, a former Naval officer, the founders of Equinox designer furniture company, took £6000 in revenue in their first year, £20,150 in their second, £63,280 in their third and £111,050 in their fourth year.

Former stockbroker, David Stapleton, was 40 when in 1977 he bought Pinneys, a sleepy salmon smoking business in the Scottish borders, for £20,000. In 1980 Pinneys made its first real breakthrough, when it secured Marks & Spencer as a customer. It was a gamble for M&S who had never stocked products costing more than £3 per lb on their shelves before. But it paid off for both of them. By 1987 Stapleton had taken Pinneys' sales to £50 million pa and an estimated net worth of £15 million.

Former advertising executive John Nettleton borrowed £1800 from his four-year-old daughter's building society in 1982 and set up his business in a tumbledown shed in Richmond. His company, Micro-Scent, use micro-encapsulation technology to trap bubbles of fragrant oil on paper. Scratching or rubbing releases the scent over time. The principal application is scented drawer lining paper.

His first year's turnover amounted to £30,000 with a nominal £1000 loss. A friendly bank manager, enthused by the venture's prospects, advanced £70,000 for proper manufacturing equipment on the basis of a business plan and £10,000 collateral on his house. In his second year turnover was £204,000 with profits at £45,000; the third year turnover was £369,000; in his fourth year turnover rose to £680,000 with profits forecast at £130,000.

Worksheet for Assignment 11: The sales forecast

1. Provide details of any firm orders on hand.
2. Provide details of all customers you expect to sell to over the forecast period, and how much you expect to sell to each.
3. Give market research data that supports or verifies these forecasts. This is particularly important for ventures in the retail field, for example, when names of customers are not necessarily known in advance.
4. Prepare a sales forecast by value and volume for each major product group (eg, for a hotel: bedrooms, restaurant, off licence) throughout the whole period of the business plan – eg, up to five years (monthly for years 1 and 2 and quarterly thereafter).
5. Support your forecast with examples from other similar ventures started recently, and drawing from company accounts and other sources.
6. Give an estimate of the likely market share that these forecasts imply.

Suggested further reading
Market and Sales Forecasting: A Total Approach, Gordon J Bolt, 2nd edition, Kogan Page, 1987.

Assignment 12
Pro Forma Balance Sheet

Before looking in detail at the balance sheet, it will be useful to see why financial data is such an important element of the business plan, and what sort of information on financial performance is needed.

The sales forecasts are the essential input from which financial projections contained in a business plan are made. These projections are not the business plan, rather they should be viewed as the financial consequences of pursuing a particular course of action. Every business plan should contain them. If additionally you can demonstrate a sound grasp of financial matters, you will be talking the same language as financiers, which has to be an advantage in any negotiation for funds. But more importantly, the financial reports used for planning the business are also used for monitoring results and controlling events once the venture is underway.

Liquidators, who ought to know why businesses fail if anyone does, have at the top of their reasons for failure: 'lack of reliable financial information'. Many failed entrepreneurs believe accounting to be a bureaucratic nuisance carried out for the benefit of the Inland Revenue alone. These same people, who would never drive a car without a fuel gauge, speedometer or oil pressure indicator, frequently set off at breakneck speed running their business with only a 'gut feel', or perhaps the annual accounts to guide them. For them the end of the first year is often the end of the business. Financiers recognise this syndrome only too well, which is one reason why they take the 'financials' so seriously. The other reason is that it's *their* money that is at stake.

Taking the analogy further, the motorist must also plan ahead to arrive successfully at his goal – to reach his destination safely and on time.

The success of any journey, particularly a long one, depends very much on the care taken at this stage. The preparation must centre around three distinct areas:

- *The car.* Making sure it is serviced, filled with fuel, and generally in a fit state to make the journey.

- *The route.* Choosing one which takes account of other traffic, possible roadworks, and *en route* facilities such as petrol, refreshments etc. You should also choose the route which is both the shortest practical route, and one with which you are familiar.
- *The travellers.* Ensuring that everyone is prepared for the journey. This may mean seeing that the children have been to the loo, and some games and toys have been packed to keep them occupied on the journey. It will also mean ensuring that the luggage is packed and loaded into the car, and the house is left secured.

If this stage is accomplished with reasonable care and attention, the travellers and their vehicle have a very good chance of success in the next phase, which is the journey itself.

The most sound approach to any journey is to calculate how far the distance to be travelled is, determine an average travelling speed that is maintainable and safe, and from these two determine the time needed to travel this distance. Working back from when you want to arrive at your destination and allowing a margin of safety for petrol stops, refreshments etc, you can calculate when you should set off.

The rest of the journey, given that Phase 1 has been carried out properly, should be plain sailing provided you follow your plan, follow the map correctly, and take account of the warning signs along the route. In all probability you will arrive at your destination safely and on time.

There are many parallels between the planning, information needs, and decisions made by the safe motorist and the successful entrepreneur's business plan as the financial reports described below will illustrate.

Balance sheet (Assignment 12)

Entrepreneurs need a method of periodically measuring the growth and development of their venture. The balance sheet is this 'snapshot' which shows where the money came from to fund his business and where it was spent at a fixed point in time, usually at yearly intervals. The 'where it came from' will usually include share capital, the profit generated to date, and loans received to date (both long and short term). The 'where it went to' will usually include fixed assets, stocks, debtors, plus the cash left in the 'tank'. The comparison with motoring would be the milometer which measures the absolute distance the car has travelled, as opposed to the relative or changing performance measurement offered by the speedometer.

Profit and loss account (Assignment 13)

This is like a moving picture of how well the business is doing in terms of sales, costs, and profitability, usually prepared on a monthly basis but covering an accounting period of one year. This can be compared to the speedometer in the car which constantly changes as the car progresses on its journey. The profit and loss account monitors the day-to-day performance of the business and gives the businessman the information he needs to identify the areas where corrective action needs to be taken – the equivalent of slowing down and taking notice of the road signs.

Cash flow statement (Assignment 14)

Yet another moving picture of how well the business is doing, but this time in terms of cash flow generation. It bears a very close resemblance to the profit and loss account but reflects the effect that credit taken from suppliers and given to customers has on cash flow. Profit does not always equal cash. Here, the comparison with the car is particularly apt: a car needs petrol to run and the petrol gauge shows how much there is in the tank; a business needs cash to survive and the cash flow statement shows how much there is in the business's 'tank'.

Break-even analysis (Assignment 15)

With the information contained in the above financial statements the businessman will know if he has made a profit or loss in the past, but he may not know whether he is still making a profit. The break-even analysis will show the level of sales required to generate sufficient gross profit to cover the overheads of the business, and thereby break even. The businessman can now be confident that if he trades at above this break-even level of sales he will be operating profitably, barring any changes in the level of gross profit and overheads. In car terms, the driver knows that in order to arrive at his destination on time he has to average so many miles per hour, say 50. If he averages less than 50 miles per hour then he will be late, and if he exceeds it for any length of time he will arrive early. In business terms arriving early equals making a profit, and arriving late equals making a loss. The 50 miles per hour is his break-even point.

Assumptions underpinning financial forecasts

These financial statements form a significant part of any business plan. However, they can only be produced once the sales forecast has been arrived at. Their believability (as well as their construction) will also to a large extent depend upon the validity of the assumptions made along the way.

An example of these assumptions is given in the extract from a business plan below:

Celtic Carveries will set up and operate a small chain of carvery restaurants in Scotland. These will provide traditional food in a relaxed atmosphere offering value-for-money food in the middle price market.

The carvery is already a proven concept in parts of England, serving roast meals on a quick throughput basis but without the 'fast food' image. Labour costs are low and with a limited menu, waste is avoided and cooking processes simplified. These factors reduce operating costs which in turn makes value for money possible.

One carvery has been in operation for six months in Stirling, so the following assumptions have been drawn partly from experience and partly from market research.

Profit and loss assumptions

(a) *Sales*
   - Carveries in operation will be:
     year 1–2
     year 2–4
     year 3–7
     year 5 onwards – 10
   - Opening six days per week, meal sales will be:
     year 1–40 per day
     year 2–50 per day
     year 3 onwards – 60 per day
   - Sales value per meal will be:
     food – £6.50
     drink – £2.50
(b) *Cost of sales per meal*
   food   £1.75
   drink   £1.00
   labour   £2.70
            ‾‾‾‾‾
            £5.45
   This equals 61 per cent of sales
(c) *Wages.* Each carvery will employ seven staff at a cost of £42,600 pa (labour costs = 30 per cent of sales which compares favourably with a general restaurant's 40 per cent)
(d) *Directors.* Paid £15,000 in first year, rising to £20,000 from year 3
(e) *Administrative staff.* Needed mainly from year 2. Costs will rise from £5000 to £40,000 over seven years
(f) *Rent and services.* £30,000 per carvery per annum
(g) *Alterations, equipment and decoration.* £40,000 per carvery
(h) *Advertising.* £2000 per carvery per annum
(i) *Inflation.* All income and expenditure is stated at current prices

169

Cash flow assumptions

(a) No debtors – all meals paid for in cash
(b) Salaries and wages paid monthly
(c) Purchases paid monthly
(d) Rent paid half yearly
(e) Rates paid monthly
(†) Loan interest paid quarterly from month 1
(g) Overdraft interest paid quarterly from month 3
(h) Sales spread evenly over each month of year (sensitivity analysis described later shows how this assumption can be varied)

Balance sheet assumptions

(a) *Closing stock*. Building up to six weeks' sales
(b) *Depreciation of fixed assets*. Improvements and office – 20 per cent per annum; fixtures and fittings – 25 per cent per annum
(c) *Creditors*. Equivalent to one month cost of sales

Let's now look at each account in more detail, showing how it can be prepared for inclusion in your business plan. We will start with the balance sheet.

Pro forma balance sheet

A personal experience

This example looks at the finances of Terry Brown. She has become a little confused by the complexity of her financial affairs and has decided to get things sorted out. In short, she wants to know where she stands.

If you were to summarise your present financial position it would contain at least some elements of the following example:

Terry Brown – financial position today (28 March)

	£
Cash	50
House	50,000
Mortgage	45,000
Money owed by sister (Jackie)	135
Overdraft	100
Car	1,000
Credit cards	50
Jewellery and paintings	350
Hire purchase (on various goods)	500
Furniture	500

This information tells us something of Terry's circumstances, but until we organise the information we cannot really understand her true financial position.

Terry believes that in money matters, things divide neatly into two: things you have and things you owe, with the latter usually exceeding the former. So, using this concept and slightly different words, we could show the same information in the following manner. On the right hand side we have made a list of Terry's *assets:* what she has done with the money she has had. On the left is listed where she got the money from to pay for these assets: the *liabilities and claims* against her.

Terry Brown – financial position today (28 March)

Liabilities and claims (where I got the money from)	£	Assets (what I have done with the money)	£
Overdraft	100	Cash	50
Mortgage	45,000	House	50,000
Hire purchase	500	Car	1,000
Credit cards	50	Jewellery and paintings	350
		Money owed by sister	135
Total claims by other people	45,650	Furniture	500
My capital	6,385		
Total of my and other people's capital	52,035	My assets	52,035

You may even have got a little lost towards the bottom of the left hand column. This is simply because we have to try to show the complete picture of Terry's financial affairs. She has acquired £52,035's worth of assets and must have provided an identical sum from one source or other. We can find only £45,650 owed to other people. The only reasonable assumption is that Terry herself must have put her past salary or wages towards buying the assets.

Now, while Terry might be happy with the help we have given her so far, it is unlikely she will be completely satisfied. Like the rest of us, she probably considers events as long or short term in nature. Even though we have shown a fairly dazzling picture of £52,000+ of assets, she knows she is short of cash for day-to-day living. So once again we could restructure the information on her financial position to give a clearer picture.

Terry Brown – financial position today (28 March)

Liabilities (long term) (where I got the money from)	£	Assets (long term) (what I have done with the money)	£
Mortgage	45,000	House	50,000
Hire purchase	500	Car	1,000
My capital	6,385	Jewellery and paintings	350
		Furniture	500
	51,885		51,850
Current liabilities (short term)		*Current assets* (short term)	
Overdraft	100	Money owed by sister	135
Credit cards	50	Cash	50
	150		185
Total liabilities	52,035	Total assets	52,035

For example, we can now see that her short-term financial position is dominated by the money her sister owes her. If that is safe, then all current liabilities can be met. If it is not safe and the money is unlikely to be repaid quickly, the position is not so good. There is an accounting convention according to which 'current' liabilities are those that we will have to pay within a year. Similarly, 'current' assets will turn into cash within a year.

We are getting very close to having a *balance sheet* of Terry's financial position. One further adjustment will reveal all. It is vital that both the long- and short-term financial positions are readily visible to the examiner. Terry's day-to-day assets and liabilities need to be clearly highlighted. What we are looking for is the net position: how much she currently owes, subtracted from how much she has.

By redrafting the financial position, we shall see the whole picture much more clearly. £51,850 is tied up in *fixed assets* and £35 is tied up in *net current assets*. All these assets have been *financed by* £6385 of Terry's capital and £45,500 has been provided by a mortgage and a hire purchase company.

The structure of the business balance sheet

The balance sheet of a business has many similarities to the personal account we have just examined. However, some of the terms used may be new to you. Returning to Celtic Carveries, let's see how a business balance sheet is constructed as shown opposite.

Celtic Carveries
Balance Sheets at 31 October

	Year 1	Year 2	Year 3	Year 4	Year 5
Net assets employed					
Fixed assets					
Improvements	48,000	86,400	141,120	184,896	147,916
Fixtures and office	30,500	43,900	82,995	97,051	85,631
	78,500	130,300	224,115	281,947	233,547
Current assets					
Stock	1,887	38,425	72,819	109,250	109,250
Cash	0	2,366	2,029	10,863	120,641
	1,887	40,791	74,848	120,113	229,891
less					
Current liabilities					
Creditors	11,383	25,617	48,546	72,833	72,833
Overdraft	6,063	27,929	60,974	45,657	0
Tax	0	4,000	25,000	58,000	80,000
	17,446	57,546	134,520	176,490	152,833
= Net current assets	(15,559)	(16,745)	(59,672)	(56,378)	77,058
Total assets less current liabilities	62,941	113,545	164,463	225,569	310,605
Financed by:					
Share capital					
Owners	15,000	15,000	15,000	15,000	15,000
Other directors	10,000	10,000	10,000	10,000	10,000
New Venture Capital	20,000	90,000	120,000	150,000	150,000
Profit/loss for year	(24,317)	(28,455)	(8,557)	25,569	85,036
Retained earnings/ reserves	–	–	–	–	25,569
	20,683	86,545	136,443	200,569	285,605
Loan capital					
Long term	25,000	25,000	25,000	25,000	25,000
Medium term	17,258	2,000	3,000	–	–
	42,258	27,000	28,000	25,000	25,000
TOTAL	62,941	113,545	164,463	225,569	310,605

First, you will notice the date at the top. This is essential, as the balance sheet is a picture of the business at a particular moment in time. The picture could look quite different tomorrow if, for example, more money was spent on fixtures. That would cause the fixed assets to rise – and the overdraft in all probability.

You can also see that some different terms are used for the account categories. Before looking at the main elements of this balance sheet it will be useful to describe the key terms, assets and liabilities.

Assets

Assets are 'valuable resources, owned by a business'. You can see that there are two key points in the definition:

1. To be valuable the resource must be cash, or of some use in generating current or future profits. For example, a debtor (someone who owes a business money for goods or services provided) usually pays up. When he does, the debtor becomes cash and so meets this test. If there is no hope of getting payment then you can hardly view the sum as an asset.
2. Ownership, in its legal sense, can be seen as being different from possession or control. The accounting use of the word is similar but not identical. In a business, possession and control are not enough to make a resource an asset. For example, a leased machine may be possessed and controlled by a business but be owned by the leasing company. So not only is it not an asset, it is a regular expense appearing on the profit and loss account.

Liabilities

These are the claims by people outside the business. In this example only creditors, overdraft and tax are shown, but they could include such items as accruals, deferred income etc. The 'financed by' section of our example balance sheet is also considered in part as liabilities.

Current

This is the term used with both assets and liabilities to show that they will be converted into cash, or have a short life (under one year).

Now let's go through the main elements of the balance sheet.*

---

*The precise layout of a balance sheet according to the Companies Act rules will be slightly different. However, this is not relevant for business planning purposes.

Net assets employed

This is the 'what have we done with the money?' section. A business can only do three things with funds:

1. It can buy *fixed assets*, such as premises, machinery and motor cars. These are assets that the business intends to keep over the longer term. They will be used to help to make profits, but will not physically vanish in the short term (unless sold and replaced, like motor cars, for example).
2. Money can be tied up in *working capital*, that is, 'things' immediately involved in the business's products (or services), that will vanish in the short term. Stocks get sold and are replaced; debtors pay up, and creditors are paid; and cash circulates. Working capital is calculated by subtracting the current liabilities from the current assets. This is the net sum of money that a business has to find to finance the working capital. In the balance sheet this is called the *net current assets*, but on most other occasions the term working capital is used.
3. Finally, a business can put money aside over the longer term, perhaps in local government bonds or as an investment in someone else's business venture. In the latter case this could be a prelude to a takeover. In the former it could be a cash reserve for future capital investment. The account category is called *investments*. It is not shown in this example as it is a fairly rare phenomenon in new or small businesses, which are usually cash hungry rather than rich.

Financed by

This section of the balance sheet shows where the money came from. It usually has at least two subheadings, although larger companies can have many more.

1. *Share capital.* This is the general name given to the money put in by various people in return for a part share in the business. If the business is successful they may get paid a dividend each year, but their principal reward will come from the expected increase in the worth of the business and the consequent rise in value of their share (more on this subject in Assignment 16).

   The profit or loss for each year is added to or subtracted from the shareholder's investment. Eventually, once the business is profitable, it will have some money left each year to plough back into reserves. This term conjures up pictures of sums of cash stored away for a rainy day. It is important to remember that this is not necessarily so. The only cash in a business is that shown under that heading in the current assets. The reserves, like all the other funds, are used to finance a business and are tied up in the fixed assets and working capital.

2. The final source of money to finance a business is long- or medium-term *loans* from outside parties. These loans could be in the form of debentures, a mortgage, hire purchase agreements or long-term loans from a bank. The common features of all such loans are that businesses have to pay interest on the money and eventually repay the capital, whether or not the business is successful. Conversely, if the business is a spectacular success the lenders, unlike the shareholders, will not share in the extra profits.

Some ground rules

These ground rules are generally observed by accountants when preparing a balance sheet.

1. *Money measurement.* In accounting, a record is kept only of the facts that can be expressed in money terms. For example, the state of your health, or the fact that your main competitor is opening up right opposite in a more attractive outlet, are important business facts. No accounting record of them is made, however, and they do not show up on the balance sheet, simply because no objective monetary value can be assigned to these facts.

    Expressing business facts in money terms has the great advantage of providing a common denominator. Just imagine trying to add typewriters and motor cars, together with a 4000 sq ft workshop, and then arriving at a total. You need a common term to be able to carry out the basic arithmetical functions, and to compare one set of accounts with another.

2. *Business entity.* The accounts are kept for the business itself, rather than for the owner(s), workers, or anyone else associated with the firm. If an owner puts a short-term cash injection into his business, it will appear as a loan under current liabilities in the business account. In his personal account it will appear as an asset – money someone else owes him. So depending on which point of view you take, the same sum of money can be an asset or a liability. And, as in this example the owner and the business are substantially the same person, the possibilities of confusion are considerable.

    This source of possible confusion must be cleared up and the business entity concept does just that. The concept states that assets and liabilities are always defined from the business's viewpoint.

3. *Cost concept.* Assets are usually entered into the accounts at cost. For a variety of reasons, the real 'worth' of an asset will probably change over time. The worth, or value, of an asset is a subjective estimate on which no two people are likely to agree. This is made even more

complex and artificial because the assets themselves are usually not for sale. So in the search for objectivity, the accountants have settled for cost as the figure to record. It means that a balance sheet does not show the current worth, or value of a business. That is not its intention. Nor does it mean that the 'cost' figure remains unchanged for ever. For example, a motor car costing £6000 may end up looking like this after two years:

	Year 1	Year 2
Fixed assets:		
Motor car	6,000	6,000
less cumulative depreciation	1,500	3,000
Net assets	4,500	3,000

The depreciation is how we show the asset being 'consumed' over its working life. It is simply a bookkeeping record to allow us to allocate some of the cost of an asset to the appropriate time period. The time period will be determined by such factors as how long the working life of the asset is. The Inland Revenue does not allow depreciation as a business expense but it does allow tax relief on the capital expenditure.

Other assets, such as freehold land and buildings, will be revalued from time to time, and stock will be entered at cost, or market value, whichever is the lower, in line with the principle of conservatism (explained later).

4. *Going concern.* Accounting reports always assume that a business will continue trading indefinitely into the future, unless there is good evidence to the contrary. This means that the assets of the business are looked at simply as profit generators and not as being available for sale.

Look again at the motor car example above. In year 2, the net asset figure in the accounts, prepared on a 'going concern' basis, is £3000. If we knew that the business was to close down in a few weeks, then we would be more interested in the car's resale value than its 'book' value; the car might fetch only £2000 which is quite a different figure.

Once a business stops trading, we cannot realistically look at the assets in the same way. They are no longer being used in the business to help to generate sales and profits. The most objective figure is what they might realise in the market-place. Anyone who has been to a sale of machinery will know the difference between book and market value!

Business name: ....

	Year 1 (19XX)			
	Qtr 1	Qtr 2	Qtr 3	Qtr 4
Fixed assets				
Cost				
Accum depreciation				
Net book value				
Current assets				
Stock & WIP				
Debtors				
Bank & cash				
Current liabilities				
Trade creditors				
Bank overdraft				
Short-term loan				
Net current assets				
Total assets less current liabilities				
Net assets				
Financed by				
Called-up shares				
Accum profits (deficit)				
Loan capital				

Pro forma balance sheets

Years ended:

Year 2 (19XX)

Qtr 1	Qtr 2	Qtr 3	Qtr 4

Business name: ....

	Opening	(19XX) Year 1
Fixed assets		
Cost	_____	_____
Accum depreciation	_____	_____
Net book value	_____	_____
Current assets		
Stock & WIP	_____	_____
Debtors	_____	_____
Bank & cash	_____	_____
	_____	_____
Current liabilities		
Trade creditors	_____	_____
Bank overdraft	_____	_____
Short-term loan	_____	_____
	_____	_____
Net current assets	_____	_____
Total assets less current liabilities	_____	_____
	_____	_____
Net assets	_____	_____
Financed by		
Called-up shares	_____	_____
Accum profits (deficit)	_____	_____
Loan capital	_____	_____
	_____	_____

Pro forma balance sheets
Summary of years 1 to 5
Years ended:

(19XX) Year 2	(19XX) Year 3	(19XX) Year 4	(19XX) Year 5

5. *Dual aspect.* To keep a complete record of any business transaction we need to know both where money came from, and what has been done with it. It is not enough simply to say, for example, that someone has put £1000 into their business. We have to show how that money has been used to buy fixtures, stock in trade etc.

Worksheet for Assignment 12: Pro forma balance sheet

Using the format on the pro forma balance sheets:

1. Construct a balance sheet for your business as it might look on the day *before* you start trading. This should be done now.
2. List and explain the assumptions underpinning your financial forecasts.
3. Construct a balance sheet at the end of years 1, 2, 3, 4 and 5 assuming you achieve the level of sales in your sales forecast. These should be done after you have completed the profit and loss account (Assignment 13) and cash flow forecast (Assignment 14).

Remember you should produce years 1 and 2 (quarterly) and years 3, 4 and 5 (annually) using the pro forma sheets with this assignment.

Suggested further reading
Financial Management for the Small Business, 2nd edition, Colin Barrow, Kogan Page, 1988.

Assignment 13
Pro Forma Profit and
Loss Statement

The balance sheet shows the financial position of a business at a particular moment in time. Over time that picture will change, just as pictures of you, first as a baby, then as a teenager and lastly as an adult, will all be different – but nevertheless true likenesses of you. The 'ageing' process that changes a business's appearance is an event called a transaction. This takes place when anything is done that can be represented in money terms. For example, if you buy in stock, sell out to a customer or take credit, these are all events that can be expressed in money.

Dealing with transactions

Let us take a very simple example. On 6 April a new business called High Finance Limited is started. The initial share capital is £10,000 and on day 1 this money is held in the company's bank. The balance sheet would look something like this:

Balance Sheet for High Finance Ltd at 6 April 19XX

	£
Assets employed	
Cash at bank	10,000
Financed by	
Share capital	10,000

Not very profound, but it does show the true picture at that date. On 7 April things begin to happen:

Balance Sheet for High Finance Ltd at 7 April 19XX

Assets employed	£	£
Current assets		
Cash at Bank A and in hand	15,000	
Less current liabilities		
Overdraft (Bank B)	5,000	
Net current assets		10,000
Financed by		
Share capital		10,000

High Finance borrows £5000 on an overdraft from another bank, taking the money out immediately in cash. This event is an accounting transaction and the new balance sheet is shown below.

You can see that the asset, 'cash', has gone up, while the liability, 'overdraft', has also risen. Any financial event must have at least two effects on the balance sheet.

On 8 April, High Finance buys in stock for resale, at a cost of £2000, paying cash.

Balance Sheet for High Finance Ltd at 8 April 19XX

Assets employed	£	£
Current assets		
Cash in bank and in hand	13,000	
Stock	2,000	
	15,000	
Less current liabilities		
Overdraft	5,000	
Net current assets		10,000
Financed by		
Share capital		10,000

The working capital has been changed, not in total, but in content. Cash has been reduced to pay for stock. However, a new asset, stock, has been acquired.

On 9 April, High Finance sells for £300 cash, stock that cost it £200.

Balance Sheet for High Finance Ltd at 9 April 19XX

Assets employed	£	£
Current assets		
Cash at bank and in hand	13,300	
Stock	1,800	
	15,100	
Less current liabilities		
Overdraft	5,000	
Net current assets		10,100
Financed by		
Share capital	10,000	
Retained earnings (reserves)	100	
		10,100

In this case cash has been increased by £300, the money received from a customer. Stocks have been reduced by £200, the amount sold. Finally, a 'profit' has been made and this can be shown, at least in this example, as retained earnings (or reserves).

The residual effect of *all* trading transactions is an increase or decrease in the worth of the business to the owners (shareholders in this case). Income from sales tends to increase the worth of a business. Expenses incurred in generating sales tend to decrease the worth. These events are so vital to the business that they are all monitored in a separate accounting report, the profit and loss account.

So to summarise: the balance sheet shows the financial picture of a business at a particular moment in time. The profit and loss account monitors income and expenditure over a particular period of time. The time intervals can be a week, a month, an accounting period, or a year. While we are very interested in all the components of income and expense, it is the result, the net profit (or loss), that we are most interested in. This shows the increase (or decrease) in the business's worth, over the time in question.

Some more ground rules

Before looking at the structure of the profit and loss account, it would be helpful to look at the accounting concepts that apply to it. These are numbered 6 and 7 to follow on from the five concepts given in Assignment 12.

6. *The realisation concept.* A particularly prudent entrepreneur once said that an order was not an order until the customer's cheque had cleared; he had consumed the product; had not died as a result; and finally, he had shown every indication of wanting to buy again.

Most of us know quite different people who can 'anticipate' the most unlikely volume of sales. In accounting, income is usually recognised as having been earned when the goods (or services) are despatched and the invoice sent out. This has nothing to do with when an order is received, or how firm an order is, or how likely a customer is to pay up promptly.

It is also pssible that some of the products despatched may be returned at some later date – perhaps for quality reasons. This means that income, and consequently profit, can be brought into the business in one period, and have to be removed later on. Obviously, if these returns can be estimated accurately, then an adjustment can be made to income at the time.

So the 'sales income' figure that is seen at the top of a profit and loss account is the value of the goods despatched and invoiced to customers in the period in question.

7. *The accrual concept.* The profit and loss account sets out to 'match' income and expenditure to the appropriate time period. It is only in this way that the profit for the period can be realistically calculated. Suppose, for example, that you are calculating one month's profits when the quarterly telephone bill comes in. The picture might look like this:

Profit and Loss Account for January 19XX

	£
Sales income for January	4,000
Less telephone bill (last quarter)	800
Profit	3,200

This is clearly wrong. In the first place, three months' telephone charges have been 'matched' against one month's sales. Equally wrong is charging anything other than January's telephone bill against January's income. Unfortunately, bills such as this are rarely to hand when you want the accounts, so in practice the telephone bill is 'accrued' for. A figure (which may even be absolutely correct if you have a meter) is put in as a provision to meet this liability when it becomes due.

With these two additional concepts we can now look at Celtic Carveries' profit and loss accounts in their business plan.

Celtic Carveries – Profit and loss account for the year to 31 October

£000	Year 1	Year 2	Year 3	Year 4	Year 5	Year 6	Year 7
Sales income	224	504	955	1,432	1,600	1,685	1,685
Cost of goods sold	137	307	583	874	976	1,028	1,028
Gross profit	87	197	372	558	624	657	657
Expenditure							
Administration	5	28	30	30	40	40	40
Rent	24	48	84	120	120	120	120
Rates	6	12	21	30	30	30	30
Advertising	4	8	14	20	20	20	20
Overheads	30	60	105	150	150	150	150
Depreciation	22	38	61	77	63	50	39
Total	91	194	315	427	423	410	399
PBIT (Profit before interest and tax)	-4	3	57	131	201	247	258
Interest	7	8	18	26	11	10	0
Taxation	-1	5	28	55	80	92	95
Directors' emoluments	15	18	20	25	25	25	25
Profit after tax	-24	-28	-9	26	85	120	138

The date at the top of the profit and loss account shows the period over which income and expenditure has been measured, in this case a year. For your business plan the earlier years should be shown in greater detail, either quarterly or preferably monthly for year 1 at any rate.

Sales income

The sales income shows the value of goods and services provided by Celtic in each year. In this example all customers have paid up at the end of their meal. If Celtic had some business clients with accounts it is quite possible that some would owe money for meals provided prior to 31 October. This sum would be included in the year's sales income (refer back to the realisation concept if you are unsure).

Cost of goods sold

You may consider that everything you have spent in the business has gone into 'making' the product, but to calculate the cost of goods sold only costs strictly concerned with making are considered. These will include the cost of all materials and the cost of manufacturing labour.

Blowing up the cost of goods sold section of Celtic Carveries' profit and loss account it could look like this:

	£	£	£
Sales			224,000
Manufacturing costs:			
Opening stock (wine and food)	0		
Purchases in period	85,519		
	85,519		
Less closing stock	17,075		
Cost of materials used		68,444	
Direct labour cost (cooks, bar staff etc)		65,156	
Cost of goods sold			136,600
Gross profit			£ 87,400

This is not a complete list of items we would find in the cost of goods sold section of a manufacturer's profit and loss account. For example, work in progress, plant depreciation etc, have been ignored to keep the example clear enough for the principle to be established.

Gross profit

The difference between sales income and cost of goods sold is the gross profit. This is a measure of the efficiency (or otherwise) of the 'manufacturing' aspect of a business. The sum is what is left to market, administer, pay financing costs, provide for future growth – and leave a profit.

Expenditure

Expenditure or 'expenses' is the general term given to all the operating costs such as rent, rates, advertising, overheads and depreciation, that are incurred in the process of running the business.

Profit before interest and tax (PBIT)

PBIT is arrived at by deducting the total expenditure from the gross profit. After that, interest charges on loans are deducted and tax is paid on the taxable profits.* Directors' emoluments, as approved by the shareholders, are then deducted and the residual sum, 'profit after tax', belongs to the shareholders.

Sensitivity analysis

While you have been realistic in preparing your forecasts of sales and related costs it is highly probable that during year 1 especially, your actual performance will not be as expected. This could be for one or more reasons, such as resistance to innovation (if a new product), over-estimate of market size, change in consumer demand, slow take-up of product etc. All these could mean that sales forecasts are significantly wrong. It is advisable to preempt any potential investor's question, such as 'What happens if your sales are reduced by 20 per cent?' by asking yourself the question first and quantifying the financial effects in your business plan. You need not go into any great detail – it is sufficient to outline one or two scenarios.

Celtic Carveries' sensitivity analysis

'In arriving at sales forecasts, estimates were made by comparison with the accounts of X Ltd who have a similar operation. If, however, these estimates were incorrect and our sales were 20 per cent lower, then turnover would be £180,000 with costs of sales falling to £110,000 and the company would still produce a gross profit at the end of year 1 of £70,000. Given a fixed cost of £90,000, our first year loss would be extended from £4000 to £20,000. This position could be largely offset by cutting the directors' pay for that year!'

Summary of performance ratios

When you have completed your pro forma profit and loss accounts for years 1–5, together with your pro forma balance sheets for years 1–5, you should prepare a summary of your business's performance in certain 'key' areas. This summary will help both yourself and any potential outside investor to compare your business's performance:

1. One year against the next, eg, has gross profit grown or declined between years 1 and 5?
2. Against other similar businesses, eg, does your business give as good a return on investment as others?
3. The ratios can be used as an aid in making future financial

---

*Taxable profits are not quite the same as the profits shown in PBIT. For example, depreciation is not an allowable expense.

projections. For example, if you believe it prudent to hold the equivalent of a month's sales in stock, once you have made the sales forecast for future years the projections for stock in the balance sheet follow logically.

This summary of key ratios should include:

Sales. Actual sales, to be used as the base figure for all other calculations.
Cost of goods sold. Expressed as a percentage of sales to highlight any increase/decrease in this key area over the period.
Gross profit. Expressed as a percentage of sales to show if this has improved or declined over the period.
Total expenditure (expenses). Expressed as a percentage of sales to indicate how well these have been controlled over the period.
Profit before tax. Expressed as a percentage of sales to show how well sales have been converted to 'bottom line profit'. Perhaps the key measure of operational performance (add back tax to profit after tax; eg, on Celtic Carveries' accounts for year 1 this is 24 + 1 = (25)).

Balance sheet ratios

Net worth. This is actual 'investment' in the business, ie share capital plus reserves, which on its own gives a valuable measure of absolute growth.

Return on net worth. This is also referred to as return on investment (ROI), and is undoubtedly the key measure of profitability used by outsiders to compare your business with others. It is calculated by taking your net profit (after tax and before dividends) and dividing this by the average value of your share capital and reserves.

Debt to equity. Frequently referred to as 'gearing', this is calculated by taking total borrowings (both long and short term) divided by total capital and reserves (net worth) and expressing the result as a percentage. This ratio is, however, a two-edged sword in that if your gearing is high (mainly financed by borrowings) potential investors will see high rewards, assuming your business performs well, *but* if you are asking a bank or similar institution for interest bearing funds then they will normally expect to see low gearing, to show a certain level of your commitment, expressed as share capital, to reduce the risk of their not being able to recover their loans.

Net current assets. This is calculated by subtracting current liabilities from current assets, thereby giving creditors an indication of your liquidity or ability to meet current liabilities when they fall due.

Current ratio. This is calculated by dividing current assets by current liabilities and expressing the result as a ratio, thereby giving an indication of your ability to meet short-term obligations as they become due. It is often refined to include only those current assets 'quickly' convertible to cash (ie excluding stocks) and all current liabilities repayable within 12 months. In this form it is known as a 'quick ratio'.

Three other useful working capital ratios which both reveal the strength of financial control in a business plan and can be used in financial forecasting are:

$$\text{Average debtor collection period} = \frac{\text{Debtors}}{\text{Sales}} \times 365$$

This gives a guide as to how long you expect to take (or have taken) getting money owed to you back in.

$$\text{Days stock held} = \frac{\text{Stock (or inventories)}}{\text{Cost of goods sold}} \times 365$$

This shows the stock level held, in proportion to your sales. This is more useful than comparing figures alone, as you would expect levels to change with increases or decreases in sales.

$$\text{Average credit period taken} = \frac{\text{Creditors}}{\text{Purchases}} \times 365$$

This shows how much credit you are taking from your suppliers. As a rough guide, if you are allowing your customers 30 days to pay then you should be looking for that credit period yourself.

Summary of Celtic Carveries performance ratios

Year	1	2	3	4	5
	%	%	%	%	%
Gross profit	39	39	39	39	39
Total expenditure	41	38	33	30	26
Profit before tax	(10)	(5)	2	6	10
ROI	–	–	–	13	30
Gearing	67	24	17	11	8

Business name.......................................

	Month 1	Month 2	Month 3	Month 4	Month 5
Income					
Sales					
Misc income					
Total income					
Cost of goods sold					
Gross profit					
Expenses					
Total expenses					
Profit before tax					
Tax					
Profit after tax					

Pro forma profit and loss statement

Year ended:

Year ... (19XX)

Month 6	Month 7	Month 8	Month 9	Month 10	Month 11	Month 12	Total for year
							[———]
							[———]
							[———]
							[———]
							[———]
							[———]
							[———]
							[———]
							[———]
							[———]
							[———]
							[———]
							[———]
							[———]
							[———]
							[———]
							[———]
							[———]
							[———]
							[———]
							[———]
							[———]
							[———]
							[———]
							[———]
							[———]
							[———]

Business name......................................

Year ... (19XX)

	Qtr 1	Qtr 2	Qtr 3	Qtr 4
Income				
Sales				
Misc income				
Total income				
Cost of goods sold				
Gross profit				
Expenses				
Total expenses				
Profit before tax				
Tax				
Profit after tax				

Pro forma profit and loss statement

Years ended:

Year ... (19XX)

Total for year	Qtr 1	Qtr 2	Qtr 3	Qtr 4	Total for year
[———]	——	——	——	——	[———]
[———]	——	——	——	——	[———]
[———]	——	——	——	——	[———]
[———]	——	——	——	——	[———]
[———]	——	——	——	——	[———]
[———]	——	——	——	——	[———]
[———]	——	——	——	——	[———]
[———]	——	——	——	——	[———]
[———]	——	——	——	——	[———]
[———]	——	——	——	——	[———]
[———]	——	——	——	——	[———]
[———]	——	——	——	——	[———]
[———]	——	——	——	——	[———]
[———]	——	——	——	——	[———]
[———]	——	——	——	——	[———]
[———]	——	——	——	——	[———]
[———]	——	——	——	——	[———]
[———]	——	——	——	——	[———]
[———]	——	——	——	——	[———]
[———]	——	——	——	——	[———]
[———]	——	——	——	——	[———]
[———]	——	——	——	——	[———]
[———]	——	——	——	——	[———]

Business name...

	(19XX) Year 1	(19XX) Year 2
Income		
Sales	_____	_____
Misc income	_____	_____
	_____	_____
Total income	_____	_____
Cost of goods sold	_____	_____
Gross profit	_____	_____
Expenses		
_____	_____	_____
_____	_____	_____
_____	_____	_____
_____	_____	_____
_____	_____	_____
_____	_____	_____
_____	_____	_____
_____	_____	_____
_____	_____	_____
_____	_____	_____
_____	_____	_____
_____	_____	_____
_____	_____	_____
_____	_____	_____
_____	_____	_____
_____	_____	_____
_____	_____	_____
_____	_____	_____
Total expenses	_____	_____
Profit before tax	_____	_____
Tax	_____	_____
Profit after tax	_____	_____

Pro forma profit and loss statement
Summary of years 1 to 5:
Years ended:

(19XX) Year 3	(19XX) Year 4	(19XX) Year 5

Business name...

	(19XX) Year 1		(19XX) Year 2	
Operating				
Sales	————	%	————	%
Cost of sales	————	%	————	%
Gross profit	————	%	————	%
Total expenses	————	%	————	%
Profit before tax	————	%	————	%
Balance sheet	————		————	
Net worth	————		————	
Return on net worth	————	%	————	%
Debt to equity	————	%	————	%
Net current assets	————		————	
Current ratio	————		————	

Worksheet for Assignment 13: Pro forma profit and loss statement

Using the format on the pro forma profit and loss account sheets:

1. Construct a profit and loss account for years 1,2, 3, 4 and 5, assuming you achieve the level of sales in your sales forecast.
2. Construct a summary of your profit and loss accounts for the full five years (annually).

   Do not forget to state the key assumptions that you have made in arriving at your figures; the reader of your business plan will not be impressed by figures plucked out of thin air!

   Remember you should produce years 1 and 2 (monthly) and years 3, 4 and 5 (quarterly) using the pro forma sheets with this assignment.
3. Carry out a sensitivity analysis noting by how much each of the following must change seriously to affect the apparent viability of your business plan.

   (a) Sales lower by x per cent
   (b) Fixed costs higher by x per cent
   (c) Cost of goods sold higher by x per cent

Summary of key ratios
Summary of years 1 to 5:
Years ended:

(19XX) Year 3		(19XX) Year 4		(19XX) Year 5	
————	%	————	%	————	%
————	%	————	%	————	%
————	%	————	%	————	%
————	%	————	%	————	%
————	%	————	%	————	%
————		————		————	
————		————		————	
————		————		————	
————	%	————	%	————	%
————	%	————	%	————	%
————		————		————	
————		————		————	

4. Construct a summary of your key ratios over the five-year period
   using the summary of key ratios sheet (above).

Suggested further reading
Financial Management for the Small Business, 2nd edition, Colin Barrow,
   Kogan Page, 1988.

Assignment 14
Pro Forma Cash Flow Statement

Cash flow/profit

Your business plan must show your clear appreciation that profit is not cash and cash is not profit. In the short term, a business can survive even if it is not making a profit as long as it has sufficient cash reserves but *it cannot survive* without cash even though it may be making a profit. The purpose of the cash flow projection is to calculate how much cash a business is likely to need to accomplish its objectives, and when it will need it in the business.

These projections will form the basis of negotiations with any potential provider of capital.

Let us look at the following example to illustrate this point.

Kensington Quick Fit

The Kensington Quick Fit Exhaust Centre has just started up, employing a young apprentice. They have to stock a basic range of spares for most European and Japanese cars. In January they fit 100 exhaust systems at an average cost of £75 each to the customer, making total sales for the month of £7500. These exhausts have cost Kensington on average £35 each to buy, and their total wages bill was £300. The company's position is as follows:

	£
Materials	3,500
Labour	300
Total direct cost	3,800

The gross profit in the month is £3700 and, after making provision for other business costs of £500 for heat, light, rates, insurances etc, Kensington Quick Fit has made a profit of £3200.

However, the proprietor is a little concerned that although he is making a good profit his bank balance is not so healthy; in fact it is worse than when he started. An examination of his operations reveals that when he buys in his exhaust systems his suppliers impose a minimum order quantity of 150 units, and since he needs two suppliers – one for the European car systems and one for the Japanese cars – he has to buy in 300 units at a time. He does, however, make sure that he has sufficient cash for his other outgoings before ordering these 300 units.

At the end of the month he has spent the following cash sums to meet his January sales:

	£
Materials	10,500
Labour	300
Total direct cost	10,800

During the month he has received cheques for £7500 and made a profit of £3500 *but* his cash at the bank has gone down by £3300, and he still owes £500 for the other business expenses. He does have 200 exhaust systems in stock at a cost of £7000, which accounts for his poor cash position, but these can only be converted into cash when they are fitted to customers' cars.

Kensington's proprietor was aware of the situation as he closely monitored the timing of the outflow of cash from the business and the inflow of cash from his customers, and he knew that the temporary decrease in his bank balance would not stop his business surviving. However, there was no escaping the fact that although his business made a profit in the month of January the most immediate result was that his bank balance went down!

The bare essentials

In practical terms, the cash flow projections and the profit and loss account projections are parallel tasks which are essentially prepared from the same data. They may be regarded almost as the 'heads' and 'tails' of the same coin – the profit and loss account showing the owner/ manager the profit/loss based on the assumption that both sales income and the cost of making that sale are 'matched' together in the same month; and the cash flow statement looking at the same transactions from the viewpoint that in reality the cost of the sale is incurred first (and paid for) and the income is received last, anywhere between one week and three months later.

Obviously, the implications for a non-cash business of this delay between making the sale and receiving the payment and using a service/ buying goods and paying for them are crucial, especially in the first year of the business and when your business is growing quickly.

Celtic Carveries' cash flow projection for year 1 is shown on pages 202–3. Cash inflows are at the top and outflows below, with the next monthly and cumulative position to date shown at the bottom of the sheet. From this we can deduce that despite a fairly hefty injection of funds, they expect to end up with an overdraft of £6063 at the year end, and a worst cash position in month 1 of £17,046. An overdraft facility of around £20,000 should be included in the business plan proposal.

Celtic Carveries: Year 1 cash flow

	1	2	3	4	5
Inflow	18,667	18,667	18,667	18,667	18,667
Owners capital introduced	15,000				
Other capital introduced	30,000				
Loan capital	42,258				
	105,925	18,667	18,667	18,667	18,667
Outflow					
Capital expenditure	90,000				
Food and wine	5,703	5,703	5,703	5,703	5,703
Wages, cooks etc	5,680	5,680	5,680	5,680	5,680
Rent	12,000				
Rates	500	500	500	500	500
Advertising	4,000				
Overheads	2,500	2,500	2,500	2,500	2,500
Administration	400	400	400	400	400
Drawings	1,250	1,250	1,250	1,250	1,250
Loan interest	938			938	
Overdraft medium-term loan interest			891		
	122,971	16,033	16,924	16,971	16,033
Net inflow (outflow)	(17,046)	2,634	1,743	1,696	2,634
Cumulative in (out) flow	(17,046)	(14,412)	(12,669)	(10,973)	(8,339)

Pre-trading cash flow forecast

Celtic Carveries' cash flow projections were made on the assumption that the business was operating at optimum efficiency from the outset. This in all probability is a simplistic view. New businesses will have a period when set-up costs are being incurred but no revenue from sales is coming in. Under these circumstances your business plan should include a pre-trading cash flow forecast, as Frogurt did in theirs (see right).

From sales

6	7	8	9	10	11	12	TOTAL
,667	18,667	18,667	18,667	18,667	18,667	18,667	224,000
							15,000
							30,000
							42,258
,667	18,667	18,667	18,667	18,667	18,667	18,667	311,258
							90,000
,703	5,703	5,703	5,703	5,703	5,703	5,703	68,436
,680	5,680	5,680	5,680	5,680	5,680	5,680	68,160
	12,000						24,000
500	500	500	500	500	500	500	6,000
							4,000
,500	2,500	2,500	2,500	2,500	2,500	2,500	30,000
400	400	400	400	400	400	400	4,800
,250	1,250	1,250	1,250	1,250	1,250	1,250	15,000
	938			938			3,750
707			881			696	3,175
,740	28,971	16,033	16,914	16,971	16,033	16,729	317,321
,927	(10,304)	2,634	1,753	1,696	2,634	1,938	(6,063)
412)	(16,716)	(14,082)	(12,319)	(10,623)	(7,989)	(6,051)	

Frogurt: Pre-trading Cash Flow Forecast

£ Month:	1	2	3	TOTAL
Cash inflows				
Capital introduced	12,000	–	–	12,000
Loans	–	30,500	–	30,500
Total inflows	12,000	30,500	0	42,500
Cash outflows				
Fixtures and fittings	6,000	7,000	7,000	20,000
Stock	–	–	4,500	4,500
Machine purchases	–	17,000	–	17,000
Total outflows	6,000	24,000	11,500	41,500
Outflows/inflows	6,000	6,500	-11,500	1,000
Balance brought forward		6,000	12,500	
Balance carried forward	6,000	12,500	1,000	1,000

Business name.......................................

	Month 1	Month 2	Month 3	Month 4	Month 5
Inflow					
Total inflow					
Outflow					
Total outflow					
Net inflow (outflow)					
Cumulative in(out)flow					

Pro forma cash flow statement
Year ... (19XX)

Year ended:

Month 6	Month 7	Month 8	Month 9	Month 10	Month 11	Month 12	Total for year
							[————————]
							[————————]
							[————————]
							[————————]
							[————————]
							[————————]
							[————————]
							[————————]
							[————————]
							[————————]
							[————————]
							[————————]
							[————————]
							[————————]
							[————————]
							[————————]
							[————————]
							[————————]
							[————————]
							[————————]
							[————————]
							[————————]
							[————————]
							[————————]
							[————————]
							[————————]
							[————————]

205

Business name.......................................

	Year ... (19XX)			
	Qtr 1	Qtr 2	Qtr 3	Qtr 4

Inflow

Total inflow

Outflow

Total outflow

Net inflow (outflow)
Cumulative in(out)flow

Pro forma cash flow statement

Year ended:

Year ... (19XX)

Total for year	Qtr 1	Qtr 2	Qtr 3	Qtr 4	Total for year
[———]	——	——	——	——	[———]
[———]	——	——	——	——	[———]
[———]	——	——	——	——	[———]
[———]	——	——	——	——	[———]
[———]	——	——	——	——	[———]
[———]	——	——	——	——	[———]
[———]	——	——	——	——	[———]
[———]	——	——	——	——	[———]
[———]	——	——	——	——	[———]
[———]	——	——	——	——	[———]
[———]	——	——	——	——	[———]
[———]	——	——	——	——	[———]
[———]	——	——	——	——	[———]
[———]	——	——	——	——	[———]
[———]	——	——	——	——	[———]
[———]	——	——	——	——	[———]
[———]	——	——	——	——	[———]
[———]	——	——	——	——	[———]
[———]	——	——	——	——	[———]
[———]	——	——	——	——	[———]
[———]	——	——	——	——	[———]
[———]	——	——	——	——	[———]
[———]	——	——	——	——	[———]
[———]	——	——	——	——	[———]
[———]	——	——	——	——	[———]
[———]	——	——	——	——	[———]
[———]	——	——	——	——	[———]
[———]	——	——	——	——	[———]

Worksheet for Assignment 14: Pro forma cash flow statement

Using the format on the pro forma cash flow statement sheets:

1. Construct a cash flow statement for the pre-trading period leading up to 'opening' day.
2. Construct a cash flow statement for years 1, 2, 3, 4 and 5 assuming you achieve the level of sales in your sales forecast.

   Remember you should produce years 1 and 2 (monthly) and years 3, 4 and 5 (quarterly) using the pro forma sheets with this assignment.

   Do not forget to state the key assumptions that you have made in arriving at your figures.

Suggested further reading

Financial Management for the Small Business, 2nd edition, Colin Barrow, Kogan Page, 1988.

Assignment 15
Break-even Analysis

Calculating your break-even point

While some businesses have difficulty raising start-up capital, paradox-ically one of the main reasons small businesses fail in the early stages is that too much start-up capital is used to buy fixed assets. While some equipment is clearly essential at the start, other purchases could be postponed. This may mean that 'desirable' and labour saving devices have to be borrowed or hired for a specific period. This is obviously not as nice as having them to hand all the time but if, for example, photocopiers, electronic typewriters, word processors, micro-computers and even delivery vans are brought into the business, they become part of the fixed costs.

The higher the fixed cost plateau, the longer it usually takes to reach break-even and then profitability. And time is not usually on the side of the small, new business: it has to become profitable relatively quickly or it will simply run out of money and die. The break-even analysis is an important tool to be used both in preparing a business plan and in the day-to-day running of a business.

Difficulties usually begin when people become confused by the different characteristics of costs. Some costs, for instance, do not change, however much you sell. If you are running a shop, the rent and the rates are relatively constant figures, quite independent of the volume of sales. On the other hand, the cost of the products sold from the shop is completely dependent on volume. The more you sell, the more it 'costs' to buy stock. The former of these costs is called 'fixed' and the latter, 'variable', and you cannot add them together to arrive at total costs, until you have made some assumptions about sales.

Breaking even

Let's take an elementary example: a business plans to sell only one product and has only one fixed cost, the rent.

On the chart overleaf, the vertical axis shows the value of sales and costs in £000 and the horizontal shows the number of 'units' sold. The

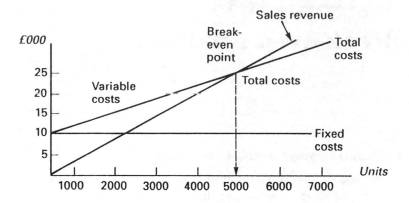

second horizontal line represents the fixed costs, those that do not change as volume increases. In this case it is the rent of £10,000. The angled line running from the top of the fixed costs line is the variable cost. In this example we plan to buy in at £3 per unit, so every unit we sell adds that much to our fixed costs.

Only one element is needed to calculate the break-even point – the sales line. That is the line moving up at an angle from the bottom left-hand corner of the chart. We plan to sell out at £5 per unit, so this line is calculated by multiplying the units sold by that price.

The break-even point is the stage when a business starts to make a profit. That is when the sales revenue begins to exceed both the fixed and variable costs. The chart shows our example break-even point as 5000 units.

A formula, deduced from the chart, will save time for your own calculations.

$$\text{Break-even point} = \frac{\text{Fixed costs}}{\text{Selling price} - \text{Unit variable cost}}$$

$$\frac{10,000}{£5-£3} = 5,000 \text{ units}$$

Capital intensive v 'lean and mean'

Look at these two hypothetical new small businesses. They are both making and selling identical products at the same price, £10. They plan to sell 10,000 units each in the first year.

The owner of Company A plans to get fully equipped at the start. His fixed costs will be £40,000, double those of Company B. This is largely because, as well as his own car, he has bought such things as a delivery van, new equipment and a photocopier. Much of this will not be fully used for some time, but will save some money now. This extra expenditure will result in a lower unit variable cost than Company B can achieve, a typical capital intensive result.

Company B's owner, on the other hand, proposes to start up on a shoestring. Only £20,000 will go into fixed costs, but of course, his unit variable cost will be higher, at £4.50. The variable cost is higher because, for example, he has to pay an outside carrier to deliver, while A uses his own van and pays only for petrol.

So the break-even charts will look like this:

Company A: Capital intensive

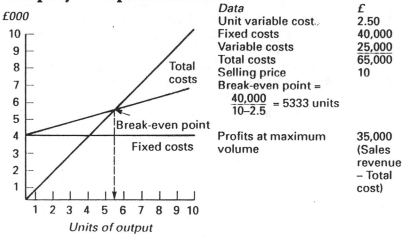

Data	£
Unit variable cost	2.50
Fixed costs	40,000
Variable costs	25,000
Total costs	65,000
Selling price	10

Break-even point =
$$\frac{40,000}{10-2.5} = 5333 \text{ units}$$

Profits at maximum volume	35,000 (Sales revenue – Total cost)

Company B: Lean and mean

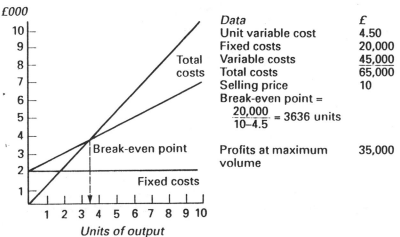

Data	£
Unit variable cost	4.50
Fixed costs	20,000
Variable costs	45,000
Total costs	65,000
Selling price	10

Break-even point =
$$\frac{20,000}{10-4.5} = 3636 \text{ units}$$

Profits at maximum volume	35,000

211

From the data on each company you can see that total costs for 10,000 units are the same, so total possible profits, if 10,000 units are sold, are also the same. The key difference is that Company B starts making profits after 3636 units have been sold. Company A has to wait until 5333 units have been sold, and it may not be able to wait that long.

This was only a hypothetical case. But the real world is littered with the corpses of businesses that spend too much too soon. The market-place dictates the selling price and your costs have to fall in line with that, for you to have any hope of survival.

Profitable pricing

To complete the break-even picture we need to add one further dimension – profit. It is a mistake to think that profit is an accident of arithmetic calculated only at the end of the year. It is a specific and quantifiable target, that you need at the outset.

Let's go back to our previous example. You plan to invest £10,000 in fixed assets in a business, and you will need to hold another £5000 worth of stock too – in all say £15,000. You could get £1500 profit just leaving that money in a building society, so you will expect a return of say £4000 (equal to 27 per cent)* for taking the risks of setting up on your own. Now let's see when you will break even.

The new equation must include your 'desired' profit so it will look like this:

$$\text{Break-even profit point (BEPP)} = \frac{\text{Fixed costs} + \text{profit objective}}{\text{Selling price} - \text{Unit variable cost}}$$

$$= \frac{10,000 + 4000}{5 - 3} = 7000$$

We now know that to reach our target we must sell 7000 units at £5 each and have no more than £10,000 tied up in fixed costs. The great strength of this equation is that each element can be changed in turn on an experimental basis to arrive at a satisfactory and achievable result. For instance, suppose you decide that it is unlikely that you can sell 7000 units, but that 6500 is achievable. What would your selling price have to be to make the same profit?

Using the BEPP equation you can calculate the answer:

---

*The UK average is around 18 per cent; high flyers aim for 35 per cent.

$$\text{BEPP} = \frac{\text{Fixed costs + Profit objective}}{\text{Selling price - Unit variable costs}}$$

$$6500 = \frac{10,000 + 4000}{6500} = £2.15$$

$$£x = £2.15 + 3 = £5.15$$

If your market will bear a selling price of £5.15 as opposed to £5 all is well; if it won't, then the ball is back in your court. You have to find ways of decreasing the fixed or variable costs, or of selling more, rather than just accepting that a lower profit is inevitable.

From the particular to the general

The example used to illustrate the break-even profit point model was of necessity simple. Few if any businesses sell only one or two products, so a more general equation may be more useful if your business sells hundreds of products as, for example, a real shop does.

In such a business, to calculate your break-even point you must first establish your gross profit. If you are already trading this is calculated by deducting the money paid out to suppliers from the money received from customers. If you are not yet trading then researching your competitors will give you some indication of the sort of margins you should aim for.

For example, if you are aiming for a 40 per cent gross profit, your fixed costs are £10,000, and your overall profit objective is £4000, then the sum will be as follows:

$$\text{BEPP} = \frac{10,000 + 4000}{0.4*} = \frac{14,000}{0.4}$$

$$= £35,000$$

So, to reach your target you must achieve a £35,000 turnover. (You can check this out for yourself: look back to the previous example where the BEPP was 7000 units, and the selling price was £5 each. Multiplying those figures out gives a turnover of £35,000. The gross profit in that example was $\frac{2}{5}$, or 40 per cent also.)

If you find that you need help in transposing the facts and figures of your business on to a break-even chart or any of the other financial statements, contact a qualified accountant.

---

*40 per cent expressed as a decimal.

Wavendon Plumbing: 12-month financial projection

1. Calculate your gross profit

Projected sales	£75,000
– Direct costs:	
Purchases (material costs)	£32,500
Labour costs	£20,000
= Gross profit	£22,500 (A)

2. Calculate your gross profit margin

    $$\frac{\text{Gross profit (A)} \; £22,500}{\text{Sales} \qquad £75,000} \times 100$$

    = Gross profit margin   £ 30 %(B)

    Note: For simplicity all figures shown are exclusive of VAT.

3. Calculate your overheads

    Indirect costs:

Business salaries (including your own drawings)	£ 6,000
+Rent	£ 2,000
+Rates	£ 500
+Light/heating	£ 500
+Telephone/postage	£ 500
+Insurance	£ 500
+Repairs	£ 2,000
+Advertising	£ 1,500
+Bank interest/HP	£ 1,500
+Other expenses (eg depreciation of fixed assets)	£ 1,500
	£
	£
	£
	£
= Overheads	£16,500 (C)

4. Calculate your actual turnover required to break even

    $$\frac{\text{Overheads (C)} \qquad £16,500}{\text{Gross profit margin (B)} \quad 30\%} \times 100$$

    = Break-even sales   £55,000(D)

5. Calculate the monthly target to break even

    $$\frac{\text{Break-even sales (D)} \; £55,000}{6}$$

    = Monthly break-even sales   £9,167

6. Profits accumulate in favour of the business once the break-even point has been reached. As overhead costs have been provided for in the break-even calculation, profits accumulate at a rate of 30% (ie the gross margin percentage) on projected sales over and above the break-even figure.

    In the case of the example, this is:

Projected sales	£75,000
– Break-even sales (D)	£55,000
× Gross profit margin (B)	30%
= Profit (for 6 months)	£ 6,000

    These figures can be affected by:

    - Actual level of sales achieved
    - Increase/decrease in gross margin
    - Increase/decrease in overheads

Returning to our earlier example of Celtic Carveries, this analysis was included in their business plan.

Celtic Carveries break-even analysis

	£
Average price per meal =	9.00
Cost of food, drink and direct labour =	5.45
Therefore, contribution per meal =	3.55
Fixed costs per carvery in year 1 =	45,000

Therefore break-even point (in meals)

$$= \frac{45,000}{3.55} = 12,676 \text{ meals per annum}$$

= 41 meals per day

Every additional £1 spent per meal lowers the break-even point by four meals per day.

Every £1 per day saved on fixed costs lowers the break-even point by one meal per day.

Achieving both of the above would turn the first year's projected loss into a profit of around £5000.

Worksheet for Assignment 15: Break-even analysis

Using the format on the break-even analysis sheet overleaf:

1. Construct a break-even analysis for year 1 of your business, using the figures from your pro forma profit and loss account as the basis.
2. Estimate the effect of the following events on your break-even point for each year:
   (a) A 10 per cent rise/fall in sales volume
   (b) A 10 per cent rise/fall in unit selling price
   (c) A 10 per cent rise/fall in variable costs per unit of sale, eg, a meal
   (d) A 10 per cent rise/fall in fixed costs
   (e) Include a requirement for achieving your profit objective by year 1 – now what 'volume' of product must you sell to break even?
3. Look back to Assignment 7, Pricing, and review your proposed selling price in the light of work/research carried out during this assignment.

Suggested further reading

Financial Management for the Small Business, 2nd edition, Colin Barrow, Kogan Page, 1988.

Name _____ Date _____

Worksheet for break-even assignment

Using the above example, calculate the figures for your own business in the space provided below.

7. Calculate your gross profit

Projected sales	£
– Direct costs	
Purchases (material costs)	£
Labour costs	£
= Gross profit	£ (A)

8. Calculate your gross profit margin

   $$\frac{\text{Gross profit (A) } £}{\text{Sales} \quad £} \times 100$$

   = Gross profit margin £ ___ % (B)

   Notes:

9. Calculate your overheads

   Indirect costs:

Business salaries (including your own drawings)	£
+Rent	£
+Rates	£
+Light/heating	£
+Telephone/postage	£
+Insurance	£
+ Repairs	£
+Advertising	£
+Bank interest/HP	£
+Other expenses (eg depreciation of fixed assets)	£
	£
	£
	£
= Overheads	£ (C)

10. Calculate your actual turnover required to break even

    $$\frac{\text{Overheads (C)} \quad £}{\text{Gross profit margin (B)} \quad \%} \times 100$$

    = Break-even sales £ (D)

11. Calculate the monthly target to break even

    $$\frac{\text{Break-even sales (D) } £}{6}$$

    = Monthly break-even sales £ ___

12. Calculate your estimated profit

Projected sales	£
– Break-even sales (D)	£
× Gross profit margin (B)	%
= Profit (for 6 months)	£

Assignment 16
Financing Requirements

Your business plan may look very professional, showing that you have a very high probability of making exceptional returns, but it will fall at the first hurdle if your funding requirements have not been properly thought out and communicated to potential investors. It is not sufficient for you to look at your pro forma cash flow statement and, taking the maximum overdraft position, say:

'The management require £150,000 to commence business, which may come either from bank loans or a share capital injection. The cash flow projections show that if the funding was by way of a loan it would be repaid within three years. If the funding came from an issue of share capital an excellent return would be available by way of dividends.'

Such a statement leaves many questions unanswered, such as:

- Why do you need the money?
- What type of money do you need?
- When will you need it?
- What deal are you offering your investors?
- What exit routes are open to your investors?

Let's examine each of these questions in turn, as your business will have to include answers to them.

Why do you need the money?

You probably have a very good idea of why you need the funds that you are asking for, but unless the reader of your business plan has plenty of time to spare (which he has not) and can be bothered to work it out for himself (which he can't), you must clearly state what you will use the funds received for.

An example might be: A net investment of £150,000 is required, which will be used as follows:

	£
To purchase:	
Motor vehicle	5,000
Plant and equipment	100,000
To provide:	
Working capital for first 6 months	75,000
Total requirement	180,000
Less investment made by (you)	30,000
Net funding requirement	150,000

This statement clearly tells the reader how the funds will be used and gives clear pointers as to appropriate funding routes and timing of the funding requirements.

What type of money do you need?

As a general rule, the greater the cost and the longer the useful life of the asset, the longer and more permanent the funding should be.

For fixed assets such funds could include:

Shares

Factories and the land that they stand on have a long life – often over 20 years – and have typical costs of £100,000 and upwards. Obviously the method of funding will very much depend on the legal status of the business: limited companies will be able to raise funds by issuing shares, either directly to the public, through a Business Expansion Scheme (BES), or via a venture capital company, eg, Investors in Industry (3i). This method of raising funds is expensive and generally only suitable for occasional funding in excess of £250,000. The real cost of this money to the borrower is not in terms of interest but in expected dividends, which of course will not be paid if the business is not making sufficient profit.

Debentures

Another option open to the limited company is debentures, which are a long-term loan carrying interest and redeemable at some fixed date in the future. These are issued in a similar way to shares, and the real cost to the company is the interest payment which must be paid even if profits are not made. Quite frequently, these debentures are secured on a particular asset or group of assets which may, under certain circumstances, be sold off to redeem the debenture if the interest is in arrears.

Long-term loans
As well as debentures, less complex forms of loan are available from clearing banks on a long-term basis. These can cover periods of up to 20 years with fixed or variable interest rates, or as a new innovation you can retain the option to switch between the fixed and variable rates every five years or so.

Commercial mortgage
The last funding option for large-scale fixed asset funding is the commercial mortgage, which as its name implies is for land and buildings. These are arranged in much the same way as a domestic house mortgage over a period of 10–25 years except that the repayments are much bigger. It is not uncommon for these to carry a fixed interest rate over the period of the mortgage, and so to the businessman this essentially represents a way of borrowing similar to the debenture, except that the commercial mortgage is available to both limited companies and other types of non-corporate businesses.

Short-term funding
Smaller and shorter-term assets, such as motor vehicles which are replaced frequently – every two to five years – are funded differently yet again. There are many more options open to both the corporate borrower and the individual businessman alike because the boom in high street lending has brought all the major banks and finance houses directly into competition with one another. The best advice for new businesses is to spread their borrowing around the various borrowing options and not to be up to their 'limit' with any one lending institution. You may not believe it but your friendly bank manager feels happier about lending you £5000 if he knows someone else is in for £10,000.

Options for financing shorter-term fixed assets include:

Bank loan
A short-term loan from your bank will usually be the cheapest, with interest charges being in the region of 1.5 per cent and 5 per cent above bank base lending rate, depending on your credit rating. While banks always like to lend money (since this is the only way they can generate income) the more commercially aware managers will suggest that for motor vehicles you should take out hire purchase or lease purchase and leave bank borrowing intact for working capital requirements for which

there is no other way of borrowing. Since hire purchase is currently very competitive this may well be sound advice.

Hire purchase and lease purchase

These have both been mentioned, but what is the difference between them? To all intents and purposes they are the same. Let's start with the more familiar hire purchase, which is a contract over a period of time, say three years, at the start of which you pay a substantial deposit (10–30 per cent) and make regular payments (usually monthly). At the end of the agreed period a final nominal sum (£1) is paid and the vehicle becomes yours. Behind the contract is the assumption that you are going to buy the vehicle.

The lease purchase contract works in much the same way. A contract is entered into for, say, three years, a deposit is made, and instalments made. However, at the end of the three years the vehicle can be returned to the lessor and the contract is at an end. Alternatively, the lessee can make a final, substantial payment, and the vehicle becomes his. The main difference is that there is no assumption that the lessee is going to buy the vehicle – his options are kept open.

Contract hire

For motor vehicles, perhaps the most common use of new business funds, contract hire is a further option. In all three financing options above the purchaser or lessee has the responsibility for taxing, insuring, servicing and repairing the vehicle as well as paying for the petrol used. For many people the costs of servicing and repairing can fluctuate quite significantly from month to month, making budgeting very difficult. For these people contract hire has many attractions.

Under this scheme a vehicle is hired for a contracted period, usually two or three years. A deposit of three months' instalments in advance is usually made, although longer prepayments are not uncommon, and regular periodic payments are made. An agreed annual mileage is determined, say 12,000, and any mileage in excess of this is charged at an excess mileage charge. At the end of the contract period the vehicle must be returned in good condition to the hire company: an assessment charge will be made if any repair work is necessary to bring it up to this condition and the hirer will have to pay this. The hirer has only to insure and put in his own petrol; everything else is included in the hire charge. Obviously this can be a costly way to finance a vehicle because the hirer pays in effect for a fleet management charge but against this is the advantage that his monthly outgoings are usually quite predictable.

Working capital

This is the day-to-day funds required to finance stocks, debtors and the like. Typically the amount of money needed rises and falls throughout the year. Funds for working capital include overdrafts, debtor factoring and trade credit.

(Further details of the different types of money available are included in the Appendix, Sources of Finance.)

When will you need it?

In the example on page 220 a net investment of £150,000 is required, which is likely to come from several different funding routes depending on how it is to be used. However, one thing is apparent: the whole £150,000 is not needed immediately or even at the same time, so don't ask for it all to be provided at the same time.

The £100,000 needed for plant and equipment will be needed several weeks or months befeore trading can begin, and the £5000 for the motor vehicle can in all probability be left to closer to the time at which you will need it. The working capital requirement of £75,000 is needed in varying amounts over the first six months or so of trading. Your funding request should clearly show this 'Timetable of Anticipated Funding'. An example of this 'timetable' might be as shown on page 222.

The statement should be carried on for as long as external funding is required, and shows that:

1. An equity investment of £100,000 is made three months prior to start-up of business and remains in the business for the medium- to long-term future.
2. A bank overdraft facility of £75,000 is required, which is first used during month 3, reaches a peak of £70,000 during month 5, and is cleared by month 9 (ie the sixth month of trading). Note that the full £75,000 facility appears not to be needed but it is advisable to obtain more than is required to cover the unforeseen.
3. An HP loan of £5000 is required in month 3, and is repaid over three years.

What deal are you offering your investors?

Clearly, you must give any potential investor 'an offer he can't refuse'. In the example we have been looking at, so far we have identified three different sources of funding, each requiring a different approach, namely:

Date	Requirement per cash flow forecast	Anticipated funding			
		Share Issue	Your cash intro- duced	Bank loan	HP loan
	£000	£000	£000	£000	£000
Year 1					
Pre commencement of trading:					
Mth 1	100	100	30	–	–
2	5		–	–	–
3	70		–	45	5
Commencement of trading:					
Mth 4	20		–	60	4.85
5	10		–	70	4.70
6	(5)		–	65	4.55
7	(20)		–	45	4.40
8	(21)		–	24	4.25
9	(25)		–	–	4.10
10	(20)		–	–	3.95
11	(10)		–	–	3.80
12	(10)		–	–	3.65

Hire purchase

£5000 is required to purchase a vehicle. This is simple to arrange, and it is not really necessary to provide a full blown business plan to secure it. This is a normal commercial transaction with low risk, short-term and scheduled repayments. Approach several finance houses, and shop around for the best deal.

Bank overdraft or term loan

£75,000 is required for short-term funding of working capital requirement. The commercial aspect of this is quite straightforward, but in this case it would be dependent entirely on two factors: the personal commitment of the entrepreneur (you) – he has committed £30,000 of his money; and the commitment of £100,000 from some other equity source. This facility/loan will need your business plan, plus an offer in writing from some other commercially acceptable source for the £100,000 equity injection. The bank should feel happy about their gearing, which is 42 per cent (75,000/180,000); also, should the equity investment fall through then their facility will be withdrawn.

With banks the following are negotiable:

(a) *Interest rate.* If your credit rating is good then stick out for the lowest rate above base rate that you can get.
(b) *Security.* If you have invested £30,000 of your own money then you have a right to refuse any request for the bank to have, say, your house as security.
(c) *Capital repayment holiday.* If instead of an overdraft you had needed, say, a three-year fixed-term loan, it would be reasonable to request an initial one-year period during which you paid only the interest. This can be vital to cash flow during the early stages of a business, and is quite common practice these days. Shop around and see what the other banks can offer you. However, do not be too quick to accept the lowest interest rate – if you think that another bank manager has a better grasp of your business and seems more sympathetic to your present and future requirements, then an extra 1 per cent on the interest rate is not such a lot to pay for this!

Equity injection

For example, the £100,000 required to fund the purchase of long-term plant and equipment discussed earlier could be funded by issuing shares – as equity capital. Most negotiations for funding are circular, with each source agreeing provided someone else comes in too. Tying up a source of equity (shares) is essential to make the other ones fall into place. All sources of equity expect to see a business plan, but before you start negotiating you need an idea of what they expect from you for their investment. Clearly, you will have to give them some of the equity in the company, but how much?

The first thing you must accept in your dealings with venture capital companies, or BES funds, is that they want to make good investments (and yours is one of these) and they want extremely high returns (35–60 per cent per annum compounded). They also want clearly defined exit routes: ie they must be able to see a way of selling off their investment in your company at some point in the three to seven-year time horizon. It will also comfort you to know that they do not want operational control of your company – they will happily leave that to you as they don't have the management resources – and they want motivated entrepreneurs. However, their lawyers will prepare a legal agreement which will ensure that while you are in control operationally, any departures from the agreed course shown in the business plan will need their consent.

It is worth just taking a little time to look at two areas of negotiating with outside equity investors which often cause concern, namely:

How much equity to give away?

For many people the valuation of companies, especially those with no track record and an uncertain future ahead of them, is a closed book. In fact, even to the professional investor it is not always straightforward, although there are certain guidelines. However, for many entrepreneurs the problems start with the idea of giving away a share of their business because they feel that they are losing control by so doing. The problem can be alleviated by looking at other successful business people who have already been down this route: Anita Roddick, founder of the Body Shop, Richard Branson of Virgin and Alan Sugar of Amstrad are all minority shareholders in their companies, yet nobody would dispute that they are in control.

People can and do sell off varying amounts of their business to raise funds. While ideally you should retain 51 per cent of the voting power in your company, it is possible to achieve this by owning less than 51 per cent of the shares. Part of the negotiating process will hinge round voting rights of shares, and it is not uncommon for outside investors to accept restricted voting rights on their shares. Don't forget that *you want their money* and you have got to give up something in return.

So far the question of how much the business is worth has been avoided, and since this is what will determine how much equity you will need to sell to raise the required funds, it needs to be answered. The formula used to calculate it is quite simple, but the factors used in arriving at the valuation are somewhat subjective. However, a simple valuation of a company by way of an example is shown below.

Cranfield Engineering Ltd

Cranfield Engineering Ltd (CEL) is a new start-up business which needs a £200,000 equity injection to achieve its business plan objectives. A brief summary of its financial projections shows:

	Turnover £	Profit after tax £
Year 1	200,000	(25,000)
Year 2	500,000	100,000
Year 3	750,000	200,000

Assuming that a P/E ratio (ie the ratio of a share's price to its earnings) of 10 is used as the accepted multiplier of earnings in their industry, then using the formula:

Present value (PV) = $\dfrac{\text{Future valuation (PV)}}{(1 + i)}$

where
FV = Maintainable profits × applicable P/E ratio
i = Required rate of return (to investor)
n = Number of years until date of forecast earnings; used to calculate valuation

Assuming that the figures provided by CEL are accepted at face value (which is unlikely) and that maintainable profits are achieved in year 2, and that our investor is seeking a 60 per cent return (because of the high risk involved), then the valuation of the company would be as follows:

$$PV = \frac{£(100{,}000 \times 10)}{(1 + 0.60)} = \frac{£1{,}000{,}000}{2.56} = £390{,}625$$

If the company is valued at £390,625 and CEL requires £200,000, then the percentage of the equity that the investor will acquire will be 200,000/390,625 which is 51.2 per cent. Obviously, while the above is mathematically correct there would be much negotiation about the acceptability of the factors being used and perhaps on which years' profits represent 'maintainable profits'. In the above example, if year 3 had been used, the investor's share of the equity would have fallen to 41 per cent.

Exit routes for outside investors

While your time horizons may be long term and your rewards partially satisfied by non-financial things – running your own business, freedom etc – potential investors are not similarly disposed. They have their own set investment criteria, outlined above, and prior to investment they must have identified an exit route within an acceptable time-scale. The most likely exit routes are:

Disposal to a trade buyer. Either your investor or the entrepreneur finds a larger company in a similar or complementary business and sells out to them. This is probably the No 1 exit method in terms of frequency, although it is not without its risks.

Share repurchase by entrepreneur(s). Whereby the outside investor is bought out by the management team, usually on preferential terms, with assisted funding. This is the least popular route, commonly regarded as the option for 'also rans' which failed to match expectations.

Public share quotation. On one of the stock markets (USM, OTC, Third

Market, full stock market). While this is the least likely route, it must be the aspiration of both entrepreneur and outside investor alike. The USM route is the most likely of the stock markets but you will need at least a three-year track record, it will cost over £100,000, and you will need to be sufficiently attractive to a wider range of potential investors. Having said that, 600 entrepreneurs have taken their companies to the USM over the past five years and become millionaires in the process. A point to remember is that in seeking a USM quotation you do not need to offer all the company's shares for sale, only a minimum of 10 per cent, so you can get rich and retain control if you want to.

The sources of finance open to you are listed in the Appendix.

Worksheet for Assignment 16: Financing requirements

Based on your financial projections, state how much cash you need to raise to set up your business, and how and when you propose to repay it.

Use the questions below as the format for your worksheet.

1. Based on the maximum figure in your cash flow forecast, how much money do you need and what do you need it for?
   £
2. How does this compare with the sum that you and your partners or shareholders are putting in (ie level of gearing)?

   $$\text{Gearing} = \frac{\text{Total funds required for business}}{\text{Money put in by you} + \text{shareholders}}$$

   For example, if you already have £1000 of assets and are looking for a loan of £5000, the funds required are £6000. If you have already invested £500 and plan to put in a further £2500, then your gearing is:

   $$\frac{6000}{500 + 2500} = \frac{6000}{3000} = 2.1$$

3. Where do you expect to raise the funds you need to finance your business?
4. Prepare a schedule showing when you need these funds.
5. How and when will any borrowing be repaid?

   Source of repayment   *Amount £*   *Date*

_____

_____

_____

Total £

6. If you plan to issue shares, how will you value the business?
7. What deal do you propose to offer to a potential investor? (Include some idea of how much equity you are prepared to sell.)
8. What exit route(s) could be open to potential investors?
9. What security, if any, is available as collateral for any loan?

Security   _Value £_

_____

_____

_____

Total £

10. Will you be receiving any grants or loans to help to finance your business (other than from the organisation to whom you are now applying)?

Source   _Date_   _Funds provided_   _Amount £_

_____

_____

Total £

11. What further private cash, if any, is available to invest in the business?

Source   *Date*   *Funds provided*   *Amount £*

_____

_____

Total £

12. What are the key risks that could adversely affect your projections? (These could include technical, financial and marketing risks.)

Risk area   *Financial impact on*
                                      Sales   *Profits*

_____

_____

_____

13. What contingency plans do you have either to manage or minimise the consequences of these risks?

Risk area   *Plan*   *Effect*

_____

_____

Suggested further reading
Financial Management for the Small Business, 2nd edition, Colin Barrow, Kogan Page, 1988.

Phase 6
Business Controls

Introduction

No one is likely to take any business proposition seriously unless the founder(s) can demonstrate at the outset that they can monitor and control the venture.

The control cycle

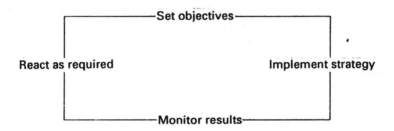

Just as your business plan should include a statement of objectives and strategy, it must also contain a brief description of how you will monitor results.

Every business needs to monitor financial, sales and market performance. Manufacturing businesses or those involved in research, development and fashion may have to observe results on a much wider scale.

In these assignments you should address the issues of importance to your type of business. If you do not have first-hand experience of working in a similar business, either find someone who has, or find a professional adviser such as an auditor, with that experience.

As a minimum, potential financiers will want to see that you have made arrangements to keep the books.

Assignment 17
Financial Controls

There are no statutory regulations in the UK governing the standard and format of business accounting and bookkeeping systems.

The various professional accounting bodies do, however, lay down some guidelines, and the auditors of limited liability companies also have standards to which they expect their clients to adhere. In any dispute with the Inland Revenue over tax, or the Customs & Excise over VAT, you will undoubtedly come off the worse without good records. Indeed, without a reliable method of getting timely information on how your business is performing you are unlikely to survive, let alone prosper. In order to get financial control you need to install a bookkeeping system *before you start trading*. Your business plan should identify how you plan to keep the books and who will do the work.

John Roberts

John Roberts manufactures traditional pine furniture, which he sells both to trade and retail outlets. During the current year his projected turnover has risen to £500,000, out of which £400,000 will be to credit customers. He reckons that his average stock holding will be £20,000 which will represent raw materials, some work in progress, and quite a substantial amount of imported furniture for renovation/re-manufacturing. He currently has an overdraft of £7000 but has a facility of £15,000 available to him. This business has the following information/bookkeeping requirements.

Daily/weekly access to:

1. Cash in the bank (or overdraft).
2. How much his customers owe to him (debtors) and for how long they have owed that money.
3. How much he owes his suppliers (creditors).
4. How much stock he has to meet anticipated sales.

The last three items can be monitored for business planning purposes using the working capital ratios described in Assignment 13.

At the same time on a less frequent basis he needs to know:

1. The profit/loss his business is making (monthly).

2. Fixed assets employed in the business (quarterly).
3. How much he owes HM Customs & Excise for VAT (quarterly).
4. How much he owes Inland Revenue for tax:

- PAYE and NI (monthly)
- business tax (monthly).

5. Formal balance sheet (quarterly).
6. Product costs and profitability.

An indication has been given in brackets as to how frequently this information is needed. You should find that your particular business has similar needs to these, but that the scale of operations may vary.

The options in this field are as follows:

Do it yourself

There is a wide range of accounting systems with pre-printed forms and instruction books available from business stationery outlets. None of these systems will work unless it is kept up regularly – which means weekly at a minimum, and preferably daily. As a drawback this cannot be over-emphasised. Unless you or one of your partners keeps a diary, a DIY system is probably not for you. Both financiers and the Inland Revenue tend not to favour this approach.

Bookkeeping services – non-accountant

You can either employ someone full- or part-time if your business warrants it, or use an outside agency. This absolves you from choosing a system or entering the information. This approach to bookkeeping will probably produce better financial controls than anything you can do yourself, and by leaving your accountant with less to do at the year end it may not cost you that much overall.

An accountant's bookkeeping system

Most successful ventures will eventually opt for limited liability status. At that stage the books will have to be audited by a suitably qualified accountant. Even businesses that don't go for incorporation, as this is called, will find difficulty in handling the inevitable disputes over tax with the Inland Revenue without an accountant's help.

So, all in all, it will make sense for most new enterprises to choose an accountant, taking local advice from banks, business colleagues and other entrepreneurs, and let him advise on an appropriate system. This will have the added advantage of being a system that can grow with your changing business needs.

Venture capitalists certainly favour having an accountant involved with the business very early on; they may even insist on putting their own on your board as a non-executive director. He would look after the investors' money – and help you to control the venture.

Worksheet for Assignment 17: Financial controls

1. What bookkeeping and accounting system have you chosen and why?
2. What control information does it produce and with what frequency?
3. Who will keep the books and produce the accounts?
4. Who will your auditors be?

Suggested further reading

Financial Management for the Small Business, 2nd edition, Colin Barrow, Kogan Page, 1988.

A Guide to Accounting Software, Kogan Page in association with the Institute of Chartered Accountants of Scotland, 1988.

A Practical Guide to Good Bookkeeping and Business Systems, John Killock, Business Books, 1983.

Assignment 18
Sales and Marketing Controls

In the early weeks and months of any new venture, large amounts of both effort and money will be expended without any visible signs of sales revenue, let alone profits. Even once the business has been trading for some time, the most reliable predictor of likely future results will be the sales and marketing efforts for the immediate past. Your business plan should explain how you intend to monitor and control this activity.

Gordon Smith set up his business, The Supreme Garden Furniture Company, in 1982, shortly after being made redundant. Using 800 sq ft on the ground floor of an old Lancashire textile mill he planned to produce a range of one- to four-seat garden benches in an authentic Victorian design, together with matching tables. Each item in the range was manufactured to a very high standard using top quality materials, such as kiln-dried African Iroko hardwood.

With professional advice he drew up a business plan incorporating cash and profit forecasts, an assessment of the market, his likely competitors, the plant and machinery required and the start-up capital he would need.

His main customers would be garden centres and he planned to spend a couple of days a week out on the road selling, initially in Lancashire, Yorkshire and Cheshire. He also produced a leaflet and price-list which he intended to send to potential customers further afield. These he would follow up later.

Smith could incorporate the sales and marketing controls shown overleaf in his initial business plan to monitor his performance:

Once Smith had gained a number of customers he found future sales to *existing customers* were much easier than constantly seeking new customers. So he kept records of existing customers, to monitor their purchases and plan follow-up visits.

Week	No of enquiries received	No of leaflets sent	No of quotations given	No of customers seen	Estimate of sales worth of week's activity

From an analysis of his customer records Smith was subsequently able to discover that garden centres in the south-east placed average orders of £2000 a time, while in his home area a £500 order was exceptional. In his business plan for his second year's trading he would be able to incorporate this information and alter his selling strategy accordingly.

Worksheet for Assignment 18: Sales and marketing records

1. Describe your records for monitoring sales activities.
2. Draw up a customer record card for your business, or show your existing one.
3. What other marketing records do you plan to keep, eg, advertising costs and results?

Suggested further reading
The Instant Business Forms Book, Roger Pring, Longman, 1985.

A customer record card for the Supreme Garden Furniture Company

Customer's name, address, phone number, key contacts and best time to phone and visit

_____

_____

_____

_____

Buying record

Date	Products bought	Value	Comments (if any)
		£	
		£	
		£	
		£	

Visit/Phone record

Date	Purpose of call	Results	Action

Special requirements

_____

_____

Assignment 19
Other Business Controls

Dependent on the nature of your venture, your business plan will have to show how you plan to control other aspects of the firm's performance. These could include:

- Manufacturing and production
- Personnel records/accident reports
- Quality and complaints
- New product development/design.

Worksheet for Assignment 19: Other business controls

1. What other business controls do you plan to introduce into your business at the outset?
2. Why do you consider them important?

Suggested further reading
Business Controls, Colin Barrow, Open University booklet, 1988.

Phase 7
Writing Up and Presenting Your Business Plan

Assignment 20
Writing Up and Presenting Your Business Plan

Up to now the workbook assignments have focused on gathering data needed to validate a business idea, to confirm the business team's capability to implement their chosen strategy and to quantify the resources needed in terms of 'men, machinery, money and management'.

Now this information has to be assembled, collated and orchestrated into a coherent and complete written business plan aimed at a specific audience.

In this assignment we will examine the five activities that can make this happen:

1. Packaging
2. Layout and content
3. Writing and editing
4. Who to send it to
5. The oral presentation

Packaging

Every product is enhanced by appropriate packaging and a business plan is no exception. The panellists at Cranfield's enterprise programmes prefer a simple spiral binding with a plastic cover on the front and back. This makes it easy for the reader to move from section to section, and it ensures the plan will survive frequent handling. Stapled copies and leatherbound tomes are viewed as undesirable extremes.

A near letter quality (NLQ) printer will produce a satisfactory type finish which, together with wide margins and double spacing, will result in a pleasing and easy-to-read document.

Layout and content

There is no such thing as a 'universal' business plan format. That being said, experience at Cranfield has taught us that certain layouts and contents have gone down better than others. These are our guidelines to producing an attractive business plan, from the investor's point of view. Not every sub-heading will be relevant to every type of business, but the general format should be followed, with emphasis laid as appropriate.

First, the cover should show the name of the company, its address and phone number and the date on which this version of the plan was prepared. It should confirm that this is the company's latest view on its position and financing needs. Remember that your business plan should be targeted at specific sources of finance. It's highly likely, therefore, that you will need to assemble slightly different business plans, highlighting areas of concern to lenders as opposed to investors, for example.

Second, the title page, immediately behind the front cover, should repeat the above information and also give the founder's name, address and phone number. He or she is likely to be the first point of contact and anyone reading the business plan may want to talk over some aspects of the proposal before arranging a meeting.

The executive summary

Ideally one but certainly no longer than two pages, this should follow immediately behind the title page.

Writing up the executive summary is not easy but it is the most important single part of the business plan; it will probably do more to influence whether or not the plan is reviewed in its entirety than anything else you do. It can also make the reader favourably disposed towards a venture at the outset – which is no bad thing.

These two pages must explain:

1. The current state of the company with respect to product/service readiness for market, trading position and past successes if already running, and key staff on board.
2. The products or services to be sold and to whom they will be sold, including details on competitive advantage.
3. The reasons customers need this product or service, together with some indication of market size and growth.
4. The company's aims and objectives in both the short and longer term, and an indication of the strategies to be employed in getting there.
5. A summary of forecasts, sales, profits and cash flow.
6. How much money is needed, and how and when the investor or lender will benefit from providing the funds.

Obviously, the executive summary can only be written after the business plan itself has been completed.

The summary below, for instance, accompanied a 40-page plan:

Pnu-Cleen will assemble and market an already prototyped design for a vacuum cleaner. The design work was carried out by myself and my co-director when we were at Loughborough University taking a BSc course in design and manufacture. The prototype was made during my postgraduate course in industrial design engineering at the Royal College of Art in London.

The vacuum cleaner is somewhat special. Its design, powered by compressed air, is aimed at the industrial market and fulfills a need overlooked by cleaning equipment manufacturers.

The vacuum cleaner offers to the customer an 'at-hand' machine that can be used by their employees to keep their workplace or machine clean and tidy during production. This produces a healthier and more productive environment in which to work.

It is cheaper than electrical vacuum cleaners and more versatile. It is also far less prone to blockage which is especially important considering the types of material found in manufacturing industry.

The vacuum cleaner can be produced at low unit cost. This, together with the market price it can command for what it has to offer, will mean that only a small turnover is needed for the company to break even. However, with the prospect of a sizeable market both in this country and abroad, the company has the chance of making substantial profits.

The company will concentrate on this product for the first five years to ensure that it reaches all of its potential market and this will make a sound base from which we can either expand into other products or incorporate the manufacturing side of the product into our own capabilities.

The financial forecasts indicate that break-even will be achieved in the second year of operations, and in year 3 return on investment should be about 40 per cent. By then sales turnover will be a little over £1 million, gross profits about £400,000, and profit before tax but after financing charges around £200,000.

Our P/E ratio from year 3 will be 10 to 1, which should leave an attractive margin for any investor to exit, with comparable stock being quoted at 19 to 1.

We will need an investment of £300,000 to implement our strategy, with roughly half going into tangibles such as premises and stock, and the balance into marketing and development expenses. We are able and willing to put up £100,000. The balance we would like to fund from the sale of a share of the business, the exact proportion to be discussed at a later stage.

The table of contents

After the executive summary follows a table of contents. This is the map that will guide the new reader through your business proposal and on to the 'inevitable' conclusion that they should put up the funds. If a map is obscure, muddled or even missing, then the chances are you will end up with lost or irritated readers unable to find their way around your proposal.

Each of the main sections of the business plan should be listed and the pages within that section indicated. There are two valid schools of thought on page numbering. One favours a straightforward sequential numbering of each page 1, 2, 3 ... 9, 10 for example. This seems to us to be perfectly adequate for short, simple plans, dealing with uncomplicated issues and seeking modest levels of finance.

Most proposals should be numbered by section. In the example that follows, the section headed 'The Business and its Management' is Section 1, and the pages that follow are listed from 1.1 to 1.8 in the table of contents, so identifying each page as belonging within that specific section. This numbering method also allows you to insert new material without upsetting the entire pagination during preparation. Tables and figures should also be similarly numbered.

Individual paragraph numbering, much in favour with government and civil service departments, is considered something of an overkill in a business plan and is to be discouraged, except perhaps if you are looking for a large amount of government grant.

The table of contents below shows both the layout and content which in our experience is most in favour with financial institutions. Unsurprisingly, the terminology is similar to that used throughout the workbook. For a comprehensive explanation of what should be included under each heading, look back to the appropriate assignments, set out in the table below.

Using the workbook assignment data

Section in business plan	Relevant assignments
1	Assignments 1 and 2
2	Assignment 3
3	Assignments 4, 5 and 6
4	Assignments 7, 8 and 9
5	Assignment 10
6	Assignment 10
7	Assignments 11–15
8	Assignment 16
9	Assignments 17–19

Sample table of contents

9. Business Controls

Financial	9.1
Sales and Marketing	9.2
Manufacturing	9.3
Other Controls	9.4

Appendices could include:

Management team biographies
Names and details of professional advisers
Technical data and drawings
Details of patents, copyright, designs
Audited accounts
Consultants' reports or other published data on
products, markets etc
Orders on hand and enquiry status
Detailed market research methods and findings
Organisation charts

Writing and editing

You and your colleagues should write the first draft of the business plan
yourselves. The niceties of grammar and style can be resolved later.
Different people in your team will have been responsible for carrying out
the various assignments in the workbook, and writing up the appropriate
section(s) of the business plan. This information should be circulated to
ensure that:

1. Everyone is still heading in the same direction.
2. Nothing important has been missed out.

A 'prospectus', such as a business plan seeking finance from investors,
can have a legal status, turning any claims you may make for sales and
profits (for example) into a 'contract'. Your accountant and legal adviser
will be able to help you with the appropriate language that can convey
your projections without giving them contractual status.

This would also be a good time to talk over the proposal with a
'friendly' banker or venture capital provider. They can give an insider's
view as to the strengths and weaknesses of your proposal.

When your first draft has been revised, then comes the task of editing.
Here the grammar, spelling and language must be carefully checked to
ensure that your business plan is crisp, correct, clear and complete – and
not too long. If writing is not your trade then once again this is an area
in which to seek help. Your local college or librarian will know of

247

someone who can produce 'attention capturing' prose, if you yourself don't.

However much help you get with writing up your business plan it is still just that – your plan. So the responsibility for the final proof reading before it goes out must rest with you. Spelling mistakes and typing errors can have a disproportionate influence on the way your business plan is received

The other purpose of editing is to reduce the business plan to between 20 and 40 pages. However complex or sizeable the venture, outsiders won't have time to read it if it is longer – and insiders will only succeed in displaying their muddled thinking to full effect. If your plan includes volumes of data, tables, graphs etc, then refer to them in the text, but confine them to an appendix.

Who to send it to

Now you are ready to send out your business plan to a few carefully selected financial institutions who you know are interested in proposals such as yours.

This will involve some research into the particular interests, foibles and idiosyncrasies of the institutions themselves. If you are only interested in raising debt capital, the field is narrowed to the clearing banks for the main part. If you are looking for someone to share the risk with you then you must review the much wider field of venture capital. Here, some institutions will only look at proposals over a certain capital sum, such as £250,000, or will only invest in certain technologies. The Appendix lists and describes the principal sources of finance for new business proposals in the UK.

It is a good idea to carry out this research before the final editing of your business plan, as you should incorporate something of this knowledge into the way your business plan is presented. You may find that slightly different versions of Section 8.5, 'The Deal on Offer', have to be made for each different source of finance to which you send your business plan.

Don't be disheartened if the first batch of financiers you contact don't sign you up. One Cranfield enterprise programme participant had to approach 26 lending institutions, 10 of them different branches of the same organisation, before getting the funds she wanted. One important piece of information she brought back from every interview was the reason for the refusal. This eventually led to a refined proposal that won through.

It is as well to remember that financial institutions are far from infallible, so you may have to widen your audience to other contacts.

Anita Roddick, the Body Shop founder, was turned down flat by the banks in 1976, and had to raise £4000 from a local Sussex garage owner. This, together with £4000 of her own funds, allowed the first shop to open in Brighton. Today, there are 87 outlets in the UK and a further 169 abroad. The company has a full listing on the Stock Exchange, Ms Roddick is a millionaire many times over – and one Sussex bank manager, at least, must be feeling a little silly!

Finally, how long will it all take? This also depends on whether you are raising debt or equity, the institution you approach and the complexity of the deal on offer. A secured bank loan, for example, can take from a few days to a few weeks to arrange.

Investment from a venture capital house will rarely take less than three months to arrange, and will more usually take six or even up to nine months. Although the deal itself may be struck early on, the lawyers will pore over the detail for weeks. Every exchange of letters can add a fortnight to the wait. The 'due diligence' process in which every detail of your business plan is checked out will also take time – so this will have to be allowed for in your projections.

The oral presentation

If getting someone interested in your business plan is half the battle in raising funds, the other half is the oral presentation. Any organisation financing a venture will insist on seeing the team involved presenting and defending their plans – in person. They know that they are backing people every bit as much as the idea. You can be sure that any financier you are presenting to will be well prepared. Remember that they see hundreds of proposals every year, and either have or know of investments in many different sectors of the economy. If this is not your first business venture they may even have taken the trouble to find out something of your past financial history.

Keep these points in mind when preparing for the presentation of your business plan:

- Be well prepared, with one person (you) orchestrating individual inputs. Nevertheless, you must also come across as a team.
- Use visual aids and rehearse beforehand.
- Explain and where appropriate defend your business concept, the product, market and your organisation's appropriateness for this venture.
- Listen to the comments and criticisms made and acknowledge them politely. You need to appear receptive without implying you have too many areas of 'ignorance' in your plans.

- Appear businesslike, demonstrating your grasp of the competitive market forces at work in your industry, the realistic profits that can be achieved, and the cash required to implement your strategies.
- Demonstrate the product if at all possible – or offer to take the financiers to see it in operation elsewhere. One participant on a Cranfield enterprise programme arranged to have his product, a computer-controlled camera system for monitoring product quality in engineering processes, on free loan to Fords for the three months he was looking for money. This not only helped financiers to understand the application of a complex product, but the benefit of seeing it at work in a prestigious major company was incalculable.
- What empathy is there between the financiers and the entrepreneurs? You may not be able to change your personality but you could take a few tips on public speaking. Eye contact, tone of speech, enthusiasm, and body language all play their part in making the interview go well, so read up on this – and rehearse the presentation before an audience.

Worksheet for Assignment 20: Writing up and presenting your business plan

1. Who do you propose to send your business plan to first, and why have you chosen them?
2. Write a first draft of your business plan along the lines recommended.
3. Who can help you to edit and rewrite the final version of your plan?
4. Prepare and rehearse a presentation of your business plan.

Suggested further reading

The Business Writing Workbook, Ian Stewart, Kogan Page, 1987.

How to Improve Your Presentation Skills, Michael Stevens, Kogan Page, 1987.

Venture Capital, the Complete Guide for Investors, David Silver, John Wiley & Sons, 1985.

The Venture Capital Report: Guide to Venture Capital in the UK, Lucius Cary, VCR, Bristol, 1987.

Appendix

Appendix
Sources of Finance for New and Small Businesses

We strongly recommend you to take professional advice before entering into any financial commitments.

The principal financiers of smaller enterprises in the UK

Source	Usual financing range £000		Total per annum £ million
	Min	Max	
Unlisted Securities Market	600	3200	270
Over the Counter	200	3200	40
Business Expansion Scheme			
Private sources	5	155	70
Funds	50	2000	40
Venture capital	50	5000+	300
3i	10	1000	320
Government Loan Guarantee Scheme	1	75	75
Bank lending	(at present around £20,000,000,000 lent)		
Local Enterprise Boards	85	100	18
Hire purchase	–	–	8000 total
Leasing	–	–	4000 total
Factoring	25,000+		4000 total
Competition	0.4	30	1
CoSIRA	1	75	–
Tourist boards	up to 50%		5
British Overseas Trade Board	–	300	–
Enterprise Allowance	2		240

British Overseas Trade Board (BOTB)
If you plan to tackle overseas markets then the BOTB, which

implements the Department of Trade and Industry's programme of export support, should be high on your shopping list. As well as free advice and information the board provides financial assistance in the following ways:

- Grants towards export market research
- Grants towards air fares for overseas trade missions
- Assistance for exhibitors at overseas trade fairs
- Help towards promotional seminars overseas
- Grants towards the cost of bringing overseas businessmen and journalists to the UK on trade missions
- 50 per cent loans, up to £300,000, to help firms to set up an overseas operation

Contact
British Overseas Trade Board
1–19 Victoria Street, London SW1H 0ET
01-215 7877
and at regional offices throughout the UK

British Technology Group (BTG)

Funded by the government, the BTG provides finance for companies and individuals who want to develop their own technology or to start up a business using products they have developed themselves. Their primary criterion is that the project should be based on a new invention, contain a significant technical innovation, or be an important evolutionary improvement on an existing product.

Over the past five years they have invested £40 million in some 300 projects all over the UK.

Contact
British Technology Group
101 Newington Causeway, London SE1 6BU
01-403 6666.

Business expansion funds

Introduced in the UK in 1983, the Business Expansion Scheme operated by these funds is designed to make it attractive for UK income tax payers to invest in new or growing businesses. Such investors must not be paid directors or employees of the business in question, nor may they own more than 30 per cent of the business.

The investor gets tax relief at his highest rate on up to £40,000 invested in any one year. In this way the investor could only have to find £24,000 to buy a £40,000 share in a business, with the tax man putting up the balance – assuming a tax rate of 40 per cent. The minimum sum that can be raised is £500 and the money must be left in for at least five years.

Accountants, bank managers and solicitors can often put you in touch with wealthy investors on the look-out for small business investment opportunities. A more likely source of such funds is from a business expansion fund. There are 60 operating in the UK and some of the principal ones are:

Baronsmead Associates Ltd
59 London Wall, London EC2M 5TP
01-638 1700

British Linen Bank Ltd
4 Melville Street, Edinburgh EH3 7NZ
031-243 8463

Cambridge Capital Ltd
13 Station Road, Cambridge CB1 2JB
0223 312856

Capital Ventures Ltd
The Priory, 37 London Road, Cheltenham, Gloucester GL52 6HA
0242 584380

Castleforth Fund Managers Ltd
150 Strand, London WC2R 1JP
01-225 2813

Centreway Development Capital Ltd
1 Waterloo Street, Birmingham B2 5PG
021-643 3941

Charterhouse BE Fund Management Ltd
Charterhouse Japhet Plc, 6 New Bridge Street, London EC4V 6JH
01-248 4000

Credit Suisse Buckmaster Moore Ltd
The Stock Exchange, London EC2P 2JT
01-588 2868

Electra Risk Capital Plc
Electra House, Temple Place, Victoria Embankment, London
WC2R 3HP
01-836 7766

Granville Business Expansion Fund
Granville & Co Ltd, 27–28 Lovat Lane, London EC3 8EE
01-621 1212

Hodgson Martin Ventures Ltd
44a St Andrew Square, Edinburgh EH2 2BD
031-557 3560

Johnson Fry Plc
Princes House, 36 Jermyn Street, London SW1Y 6DT
01-439 0924

Lazard Development Capital Funds
Lazard Development Capital Ltd, 44 Baker Street, London W1M 1DH
01-935 2731

Mercia Venture Capital Ltd
126 Colmore Row, Birmingham B3 3AP
021-223 3404

Oakland Capital Management Plc
Ramsbury House, High Street, Hungerford, Berks RG7 0LY
0488 83555

Clearing banks

The clearing banks, as the major high street banks are more officially known, are the principal source of finance, providing over £20 billion of financing for smaller firms in the UK. Through wholly or partially owned subsidiaries they cover virtually every aspect of the financial market. Their two principal products are overdrafts, which are short-term flexible financial arrangements to help people to meet day-to-day expenses; and term loans for anything up to 20 years on fixed or variable rates of interest to finance capital expenditure such as buildings, equipment, research and development and motor vehicles.

They also offer bill financing, factoring, leasing and Government Loan Scheme Funding which are all separately covered in this guide. Most people think only of the big four when they think of banks, but there are over a dozen who can help new and small businesses with their financing requirements, with over 34,000 local outlets between them.

Competitions

Competitions are one of the few absolutely free sources of money open to you. Over £1 million a year is given away in this manner, to people in Britain with soundly based business ideas. These competitions are usually sponsored by banks, local councils and big companies, offering

Clearing banks and their services for small businesses

Name	No of branches	Small business section	Government Loan Guarantee Scheme	Venture capital provision	Export/ Import service	Franchise finance scheme
Allied Irish 01-588 0691	60	No	Yes	No	Yes	No
Bank of Scotland 031-229 2555	544	No	Yes	Yes	Yes	No
Barclays 01-248 9155	2,900	Yes	Yes	Yes	Yes	Yes
Clydesdale 041-248 7070	380	No	Yes	Yes	Yes	Yes
Co-operative 061-832 3456	80*	Yes	Yes	No	Yes	No
Lloyds 01-626 1500	2,300	Yes	Yes	No	Yes	Yes
Midland 01-606 9911	2,195	Yes	Yes	Yes	Yes	Yes
National Giro 01-600 6020	20,000	No	No	No	No	No
National Westminster 01-726 1000	3,200	Yes	Yes	Yes	Yes	Yes
Royal Bank of Scotland 031-556 8555	900	Yes	Yes	Yes	Yes	Yes
Trustee Savings Bank 01-623 5266	1,250**	No	Yes	Yes	Yes	No
Yorkshire 0532 441244	228	No	Yes	No	Yes	No

*They have 4000 small outlets in shops etc.

**England and Wales only.

prizes ranging from a few hundred pounds up to £30,000. The prize will also probably include a package of help and advice and, dependent on the nature of the sponsoring organisation, a useful piece of business equipment such as a micro-computer or a rent-free work unit.

These competitions are usually announced in the press. Regular sponsors of such events include:

Sponsor	Competition	Prize Fund £
Bank of Ireland	Start Your Own Business	30,000
Churchill College, Cambridge	Small Business Essay Prize (3000 awards)	400
Daily Telegraph and National Westminster Bank	Business Venture Award	20,000
Design Council	Design Award for Small Firms	10,000
Lloyds Bowmaker and Accountancy Age	National Award for Small Business	25,000

Crafts Council

The Council, which is a registered charity working for the Minister of Arts, offers business advice to artists, craftsmen and women, as well as providing a subsidy for craft projects. They have a 'setting up scheme' to help with the cost of setting up a first workshop.

Contact
Crafts Council
8 Waterloo Road, London SW1Y 4AU
01-930 4811

The Department of Trade and Industry (DTI)

The DTI offers industry and commerce direct support through its recently announced Enterprise Initiative. More than £250 million has been committed over the next three years to helping companies in seven key areas for business success:

Business planning

Marketing
Quality
Manufacturing systems

Exporting
Design
Financial information systems

The Initiative is designed to help small- and medium-sized companies (with up to 500 employees) to use professional consultants with specific skills and experience in these key areas. Up to 30 days of professional consulting help in the designated areas can be provided, with the government paying half the cost, or two-thirds if your company is in an Assisted Area or an Urban Programme Area.

Their booklet, The Enterprise Initiative, explains these schemes and gives the contact point for each.

Contact
The Department of Trade and Industry
0800 500 200 for a free copy of the booklet

Development agencies and boards
Development agencies were set up in 1976 in Scotland (the Scottish Development Agency) and Wales (the Welsh Development Agency) by the government of the day, to coordinate and encourage all activities relating to new and small business.

Since then, similar agencies have been set up elsewhere in the UK and they are now a significant source of start-up and development capital.

Contact
Highlands and Islands Development Board
Bridge House, 27 Bank Street, Inverness IV1 1QR
0463 234171

Local Enterprise Development Unit
Lamont House, Purdy's Lane, Newtownbreda, Belfast BT8 4TB
0232 691031

Mid-Wales Development Board
Ladywell House, Newtown, Powys SY16 1JB
0686 26965

Scottish Development Agency
Small Business Division, Roseberry House, Haymarket Terrace, Edinburgh EH12 5EZ
031-337 9595

Welsh Development Agency
Treforest Industrial Estate, Pontypridd, Mid Glamorgan CF37 5UT
044-385 2666

Discount houses

These are the specialist institutions that provide, among other services, a Bill financing facility. The Bill, or Bill of Exchange to give it its full title, was introduced over 200 years ago and has flourished ever since.

A Bill works rather like a post-dated cheque which can be sold to a third party for cash, but at a discount. Once you have despatched the goods concerned to your customer you can draw up a Bill to be accepted by him on a certain date. This, in effect, is a commitment by him to settle his account on that date and not before. You can then sell this Bill to a bank or discount house and receive immediate cash. Of course, you have to pay for this service. Payment takes the form of a discount on the face value of the Bill, usually a sum directly related to the creditworthiness of your customer.

It has several advantages as a source of short-term finance. First, it is usually competitive with bank overdrafts. Second, you can accurately calculate the cost of financing a transaction because the discount rate is fixed irrespective of interest rate fluctuations. Third, by using Bill financing you can free your overdraft facility for other purposes. Finally, because they are self-liquidating, Bills are usually provided on an unsecured basis, normally only calling for a negative pledge – that is, agreeing not to pledge your assets elsewhere without the discount house's consent.

The average value of a Bill of Exchange is around £25,000, although many Bills are for as little as £2000. We know of at least one person who started his business from scratch on the basis of a Bill of Exchange on a major client for his first order.

Contact
The London Discount Market Association
39 Cornhill, London EC3V 3NU
01-623 1020

Enterprise agencies

Under the umbrella of Business in the Community, a nationwide network of some 300 local Enterprise Agencies provides both advice and funds for new and small businesses. Several of the major enterprise agencies operate 'marriage bureaux' that put prospective investors in contact with entrepreneurs searching for funds.

Contact
Business in the Community
227a City Road, London EC1V 1LX
01-253 3716

Factoring companies

Factoring is debtor finance, designed to provide liquid funds to companies with cash tied up in outstanding invoices. The factoring company takes on responsibility for the client's invoices, both issuing and collecting them, and advances money to the client against the sums due. Usually, up to 80 per cent of the invoices' value may be advanced immediately to the client company once an invoice has been issued to the debtor, with the balance (minus service charges) being paid either on the invoice being settled or after a fixed period. The factor provides credit cover against the possibility of bad debts, and bills carry the factor's name.

Factoring companies are fond of describing their service as similar to an overdraft facility; this is because it too is flexible in providing funds, and indeed sums advanced under factoring can increase in line with the amount of business the client does.

To be suitable for factoring, a company should usually be young (under about seven years old), under-capitalised and with an annual turnover of at least £250,000 - although some factors will take on companies with smaller turnovers. In addition, it should have reliable, creditworthy customers. Factoring companies have been working hard to throw off their image as last-ditch lenders, and stress that they are not interested in failing businesses but in up-and-coming ones with good growth potential.

Contact
Association of British Factors
Hind Court, 147 Fleet Street, London EC4A 2BU

Association of Invoice Factors
Northern Bank House,
109–113 Royal Avenue, Belfast BT1 1FF
0232 224522

Finance houses

Finance houses are the main providers of hire purchase funds. They were first formed in 1890 to supply credit to private traders, mainly colliery owners and coal merchants, to enable them to buy railway wagons to transport their goods. Hire purchase is now used to finance the purchase of most types of business asset and over £8 billion is currently lent in this way. Sixty of the 100 largest UK enterprises and 45 per cent of all small firms are regular users of hire purchase facilities.

Contact
The Finance Houses Association
18 Upper Grosvenor Street, London W1X 9PB
01-491 2783

Government Loan Guarantee Scheme

To be eligible for this type of loan a proposition must have been looked at by an approved bank and considered viable, but it should not be a proposition that the bank itself would normally approve. Those eligible include sole traders, partnerships, co-operatives or limited companies wanting funds to start up or expand.

The loans can be for up to £75,000 and repayable over two to seven years. It may be possible to delay paying the capital element for up to two years; however, interest payments must be kept up from the outset.

Your bank, once it receives your application, simply passes it on to the Department of Employment for their approval. Once that has been given the bank lends you the money at its overdraft rate and the government adds on a 2.5 per cent insurance premium. This is used to refund the bank up to 70 per cent of the advance if you cannot pay up.

Over 30 banks now operate the scheme and some 15,000 loans have been made totalling £500 million. The average loan has been a consistent £33,000, with about half going to start-ups.

In January 1988 the Government made it easier for small businesses to make use of the scheme by allowing banks to approve loans of up to £15,000 without further reference.

Contact
Any major bank

Leasing companies

Leasing is a major source of finance for new enterprise, providing over £4 billion a year of funding for everything from aircraft to typewriters. Operating leases are taken out where you plan to use the equipment in question for less than its full economic life – for example, a car, photocopier or vending machine. The lessor takes the risk of the equipment becoming obsolete and assumes responsibility for repairs, maintenance and insurance. As you, the lessee, are paying for this service, it is more expensive than a finance lease where you lease the equipment for most of its economic life and maintain and insure it yourself.

Leases can normally be extended, often for fairly nominal sums, in the later years.

The obvious attractions of leasing are that no deposit is needed, leaving your capital available for use elsewhere in the business. Also, the cost of leasing is known from the outset, making forward planning simpler.

Contact
The Equipment Leasing Association
18 Upper Grosvenor Street, London W1X 6PB
01-491 2783

Local Enterprise Boards (LEBs)

LEBs main funding comes from so-called Section 137 money, ie the right of metropolitan counties to spend up to a 2p rate on discretionary purposes under Section 137 of the Local Government Act.

Using this facility they lend and invest funds in new and small businesses within their own area. The boards are based in West Yorkshire, Lancashire, West Midlands, Greater London and Greater Manchester.

Most local councils have some scheme to help small firms with financing enterprise so it is worth finding out what is going on in your area.

Contact
The Industrial Development Officer (IDO) of your Local Council

Training Commission (formerly the MSC)

They introduced the Enterprise Allowance Scheme to help unemployed people to set up their own businesses in 1982. Since then over 200,000 people have entered the scheme and it has been accelerated to accept up to 120,000 applicants a year.

The Enterprise Allowance provides £40 per week for the first year, while you are setting up a business, together with a small amount of training and advice. The scheme is open to people who:

- Are receiving unemployment or supplementary benefit
- Have been unemployed for at least eight weeks
- Are over 18 and under retirement age
- Have at least £1000 to invest in the business
- Agree to work full time in the business (at least 36 hours per week)

The business you plan to set up should be:

- New. If you have already started up you are ineligible.
- Independent. You should not be a subsidiary of or be supported by another business.

263

- Small. Applications will not be accepted from people who intend to employ more than 20 people in the first three months.

Contact
Your local Jobcentre has full details of the scheme

Merchant banks
These are British banks which concentrate on advising companies and entrepreneurs on raising new capital and about buying and selling businesses. Formerly they were a fairly aloof bunch, often still run by the families that launched the banks in the 18th and 19th centuries as the financial arms of the big trading houses. These days many of them set out aggressively both to market their products and poach clients from their competitors. They are unlikely to be interested in propositions for amounts less than £50,000 but they are always worth a try.

Most merchant banks are members of the Accepting Houses Committee, an exclusive bankers club formed in 1914. A list of members can be obtained from The Accepting Houses Committee, 101 Cannon Street, London EC4N 5BA, 01-283 7332.

Private individuals
You could advertise directly yourself for backers in the quality financial press such as the *Financial Times* (Tuesdays in particular) and the *Sunday Times* Business to Business section. Alternatively, Venture Capital Report (based in Henley on Thames) and the London Enterprise Agency publish magazines putting entrepreneurs in search of funds in touch with potential investors.

Rural Development Commission (formerly CoSIRA)
The Rural Development Commission is a government agency whose objective is to revitalise country areas in England by helping to establish small rural firms and to encourage existing ones to become more prosperous. 'Rural' is defined as an area with less than 10,000 inhabitants.

The Commission normally expect the major part of your funding to be arranged with a commercial lending source. However, they have a limited loan fund which can be used to finance part of the costs of a project, up to a maximum of £75,000 over a two- to twenty-year period.

They can also provide grants towards the cost of converting buildings of all descriptions into workshops, including the cost of installing or upgrading mains services.

Contact
Rural Development Commission
141 Castle Street, Salisbury, Wiltshire SP1 3TP
0722 336255
(and county offices throughout England)

Stock exchanges

There are now three markets in operation in the UK that can help you to raise new capital to start up a business or to expand. The main Stock Exchange is unlikely to be of much interest to you unless your business is valued at over half a million pounds, you have a satisfactory five-year track record and you already have at least 100 shareholders. Over 3000 companies meet these criteria and this market raises about £6 billion a year for industry.

The Unlisted Securities Market (USM) has much less exacting requirements and since its launch in 1980 over 1000 companies have raised sums ranging between £130,000 and £247 million each. In the process over 100 entrepreneurs a year are made paper millionaires.

Finally, the Over the Counter (OTC) market is a haven that many small firms arrive at after exhausting the round of merchant banks and venture capitalists. The market is run by a dozen or so licensed dealers, who operate by telephone, matching buyers and sellers. There are now over 200 companies on the OTC, which although requiring a less stringent pedigree than either of the other stock markets, provides most of the advantages in prestige and money. It's not a cheap way to raise money – one dealer quotes £25,000 to raise £100,000 – but once you have raised the money it is interest free. You only pay dividends on this type of capital when you make a profit.

Contact
The Stock Exchange
Throgmorton Street, PO Box 119, London EC2P 2BT
01-588 2355

Tourist boards

One of the tourist boards' principal tasks is to encourage the growth of enterprise within the tourist business generally. This is done by providing a mixture of loans, grants and advice. Grants can be up to 50 per cent of the capital cost of the project, although in practice they are usually in the region of 25–30 per cent. To encourage private sector finance the tourist boards can also offer interest relief grants for certain projects.

In the past decade the English Tourist Board alone has provided £25

265

million of finance to back new projects.

Contact
English Tourist Board
Thames Tower, Black's Road, Hammersmith, London W6 9EL
01-846 9000

Scottish Tourist Board
23 Ravelstone Terrace, Edinburgh EH4 3EU
031-332 2433

Welsh Tourist Board
Brunel House, 7 Fitzalan Road, Cardiff CF2 1UY
0222 499909

Northern Ireland Tourist Board
River House, 48 High Street, Belfast BT1 2DS
0232 231221

Venture capital firms
There are now over 100 institutions in the UK that are prepared to back risky industrial and commercial ventures at the beginning of their lives. These venture capital firms invest over £300 million a year in new and small businesses for activities that range between pre-start-up research to late stage development.
   Venture capital uses:

Stage	%
Pre-start-up	9
Start-up	25
Early stage development	28
Late stage development	26
Management buy out	10
	100*

Over 50 providers of venture capital are members of the British Venture Capital Association, formed in 1983 to help to further the provision of such financing in the UK.
   Established in 1945 by the Bank of England and the major clearing banks, Investors In Industry (3i) is the largest provider of venture capital in the UK, with stakes in over 5000 businesses.

*The percentages have been rounded up or down, and the total therefore comes only to 98.

Contact
British Venture Capital Association
c/o Arthur Andersen & Co, 1 Surrey Street, London WC2R 2PS
01-836 5702

Investors In Industry (3i)
91 Waterloo Road, London SE1 8XP
01-928 7822

The Venture Capital Report Guide to Venture Capital in the UK, published by
VCR Bristol annually, describes the investment criteria and preferences
of all UK sources of venture capital.

Index